Acknowledgements

The author, being of sound mind and body, wishes to give thanks and praise to the following saintly individuals* for their support and encouragement during this book's long and troubled gestation.

Martin Corless. Mary, Ivan and Anne Marie. Jack Broder, Declan Burke and all at *In Dublin*. Ian O'Doherty. Ashlinn D'Arcy. Kevin Hamilton. John Ryan (*Scraps* of inspiration). The incredibly obliging staff of the Gilbert Library, Dublin.

And lastly, I just want to say hello to anyone who knows me.

* Thanks a million, but don't expect a free copy.

Collectors Edition #

1 7 8 9

Contents

THE SCREWS WERE ALL ASTOUNDED

Official Ireland Vs. "The Helicopter Song" 1973

The Austerity Christmas of 1973 put a full-stop on a decade of Irish economic boom. The first of the great oil crises was biting deep, and short measures were the order of the day. The three-day working week had arrived. People queued for rationed petrol. Late night TV was deemed an extravagance so RTE scrapped a lump of its Christmas schedule. School holidays were extended by a week to save the state fuel. At a time of enforced absences, Ireland's unique contribution to the global missing list was a huge hit.

Some background. Mountjoy Prison was in the news throughout 1973. In the spring, two prisoners escaped over an exercise yard wall. Then, in July, a routine garda patrol surprised a gang about to throw a rope ladder into the same yard. The men got away. A summer of riots and hunger strikes ensued, as prisoners agitated for political status. An uneasy peace was restored when the authorities allowed that the Republican prisoners would take care of their own wing of the prison.

It was the calm before the storm. In mid-October a man with an American accent phoned Irish Helicopters at Dublin Airport. Giving his name as Paul Leonard, the man - who claimed to be a movie producer - arranged to take aerial photos of monuments in Co. Laois, followed by a sight-seeing jaunt over Wicklow. On Tuesday October 30th, Leonard - "a prosperous looking man in his mid-twenties" - called to Irish Helicopters and selected their most manoeuvrable aircraft, the Alouette 2.

The exotic stranger returned the following day for his £80-an-hour trip. As arranged, the helicopter flew to Stradbally, Co. Laois, where it landed in a field belonging to Tommy Kelly, a bachelor farmer. Two men emerged from nearby trees and notified the pilot of a change of plan at gunpoint. "Mr. Leonard" departed with one of the men, advising the pilot that if he knew what was good for him he would do what he was told.

The helicopter's new passenger gave directions for Mountjoy. It was still bright when the aircraft set down in the exercise compound at 3.35pm, just as a group of Republican inmates

1

were stretching their legs. Seamus Twomey, J. B. O'Hagan and Kevin Mallon hopped on board while the other prisoners formed a protective cordon around the helicopter.

The prison staff seemed mesmerised by the whirring blades. "Some of them shouted to the warders at the main gate to lock it," testified a man visiting at the time. He witnessed "a huge cheer from the prisoners" as the craft took off. Within ten minutes the fugitives were hopping into a stolen taxi at Baldoyle Racecourse.

Meanwhile, back at Mountjoy shellshocked warders compared notes. It emerged that some guards assumed the helicopter was an Army chopper come to pick up a sick prisoner. At least one warder thought that the visitation was the Minister For Defence making a surprise inspection. As the apparition hovered the guard muttered, "Nobody tells me anything around here."

The country was convulsed, mostly with laughter. It would be months yet before the Dublin and Monaghan bombings brought the bloody reality of the Troubles down South. There was a broad consensus that Robin Hood had put one over on the nasty Sheriff. The *Irish Times* reported a scintillating new joke sweeping through Leinster House. Q: "Tell me, d'ye think it would have happened if Fianna Fail was in power?" A: "Not bloody likely! Twomey and the boys wouldn't be in the Joy in the first place." An emergency cabinet meeting appeared to conclude that the audacious break-out was just one of those things. "They regard it as something unlikely to happen a second time," surmised one reporter.

Checkpoints cris-crossed Dublin. Gardai suspected that Twomey, the most wanted of the three, was holed up in the capital. He was a slippery customer. British soldiers had once raided a Belfast house looking for him. After a fruitless search they'd apologised to the disguised villain for any disturbance caused.

Ten days after the escape, Mountjoy's Republican prisoners were transported to the high-security jail in Portlaoise. Kevin Mallon trailed his former cellmates to the town. He was having a ball at the Hotel Montague's GAA dance when an observant off-duty garda pooped his party.

It's not known whether Mallon was at the dance long enough

to join in the raucous chorus of the country's Number One hit. Performed by The Wolfe Tones it was called "Up And Away (The Helicopter Song)". The record's execution had been as speedy and slick as the feat of criminal derring-do it celebrated. A mere twenty-two days after the great escape, "Up And Away" crashed into the Top Ten. Its potent combination of topicality and cutting edge technology (a whirring-noise sound effect) quickly airlifted the song to the top of the charts.

The tune was dismal, but the lyrics combined a strong narrative with that rarest of qualities in Irish rebel songs - a happy ending. The result was a jarring mid-air collision between "Boolavogue" and "Chitty Chitty Bang Bang". All together now ...

On the last day of October in the year of '73
In Mountjoy Jail three rebels were longing to be free
When from the skies, surprise, surprise
An iron bird did fall
And lifted up the Provies and took them over the wall
And it's up and up and higher the helicopter flew
High over the Dubbalin spires and over the Liffey too
The length and breadth of Ireland, no finer sight to see
The day the Provie birdie released the Mountjoy three
The screws were all astounded, they knew not what to do
They just stood there dumbfounded, as off the rebels flew
And in the Dail the traitors were shocked and quite aghast
When they looked up and noticed the Provies flying past
O'Hagan, Twomey, Mallon, god bless those gallant three
Cruel Britain she is furious to see our adults free
But everywhere in Ireland, wherever the news is heard
The people cheer the Provies and their marvellous flying bird

The Mountjoy escape had been an acute embarrassment to the authorities. This was insult heaped upon injury - the solemn offices of the state made an all-singin', all-dancin' laughing stock. Piqued, Official Ireland reacted the only way it knew how and banned the cursed thing. For weeks, Larry Gogan's Top 30 countdown climaxed with the No.2 hit in the land. Newspapers were scrawny because newsprint was scarce, but lack of space wasn't why a most newsworthy phenomenon got zero coverage in the nationals.

Needless to say, the blanket ban increased the disc's outlaw cachet and sales soared accordingly. Soon, every ballad group in the land were featuring the toe-tappin', knee-cappin' "Up And Away" in their set. The song was recorded by several acts, eventually getting temporary release on an album entitled "The Lid Of Me Granny's Bin". Future singles by The Wolfe Tones included a dirge articulating Ireland's territorial claim to Rockall and a timely intervention into the Falklands War on the side of Argentina.

More than a decade after the runaway success of "Up And Away", The Wolfe Tones' Derek Warfield glumly reflected that "our audience in the North now would be 99% Nationalist. It's totally gone that way now, which is a tragedy." Explanations on a postcard, please. Best entry wins a copy of the seminal Sixties Wolfe Tones' album "Rifles Of The IRA".

THE BISHOP REQUESTS YOU DO NOT ATTEND

The Bishop Of Kerry Vs. Jayne Mansfield 1967

There was only one contender for Kerry Joke Of The Year, 1967. It was the one about the bishop and the actress.

Jayne Mansfield's Hollywood career had been on the skids for some time when she signed up for a one night stand in Tralee's Mount Brandon Hotel. The booking immediately divided the town's Urban Council. Councillor Michael O'Regan sounded a dire warning. "This is not the proper person we should have entertaining here," he thundered. "The lady says she cannot sing or dance, but is a sex symbol."

By the time the great day arrived, the issue of whether Ms. Mansfield's celebrated sexiness was appropriate to Tralee had escalated into a heated national debate. The promoters were confident that 3,000 paying punters would settle the matter in their favour. Their reverie was punctured by a twin-pronged jab of divine intervention. The Bishop of Kerry asked only the unquestioning obedience of his flock. His pithy message to mass-goers on the morning of the planned show was polite but firm: "Our attention has been drawn to an entertainment in Tralee tonight. The Bishop requests you do not attend."

If persuasion was needed, the Dean of Kerry followed up with the hard evidence. He quoted the siren's own words. "I am a sexy entertainer," she had said. The Dean continued, "I appeal to the men and girls of Tralee to disassociate themselves from this attempt to besmirch the name of our town for the sake of filthy gain. I ask all our people to ignore the presence of this woman and her associates. They are attempting something that is contrary to the moral teaching of our faith, that is against our traditions and against the ordinary decencies of life, something that is against everything we hold dear."

Worse still, according to the Dean, the very presence of this particular Catholic mother of five in the town would cast a slur on the annual Festival Of Kerry - the self same jamboree that each year selected one maiden as an ideal of womanhood and honoured her as Rose Of Tralee. The Dean knew that he would be accused of provincialism, but what was wrong with that? He pointed out that in Jerusalem they'd said of Jesus: "What do you expect from him? He comes from Nazareth." The Dean stressed that he was not an intellectual, but he knew that if his parishioners worshipped Christ in the morning, they could not play with the Devil in the evening.

That same afternoon the placebo Monroe met the press at Dublin Airport while she awaited her transfer to Shannon. Caressing the mandatory pet Chihuahuas with rhinestoned fingers, the emerald-garbed star presented a pair of impeccable credentials - she never missed Sunday mass and she'd been Queen of the previous month's Saint Patrick's Day parade in Sacramento, California. "I wore a green mini-skirt", she smouldered.

Informed of the Bishop's ruling of that morning, Jayne declared herself "quite surprised". "My show is not risqué," she insisted. "It's satirical. My clothes will be tight-fitting but high-necked, especially because it's Sunday. I think it's much more elegant, and sexier, to be fully clothed." She outlined an alternative theory for the cleric's hostility. "I did make a big mistake once," she giggled, "and maybe the Bishop remembers." It transpired that on her first visit to Ireland, eight years previously, she'd remarked fawningly upon the beauty of her "British" surroundings.

A huge crowd of well-wishers awaited Mansfield at Shannon. "Isn't it wonderful," she gushed, leaning against a counter to take in the scene. Within minutes of her chauffeured departure, an Aer Lingus clerk had erected a sign on the counter proclaiming "JAYNE RESTED HERE". When the star vehicle caught a flat near the town of Castleisland, Jayne made straight for the only place open on a Sunday afternoon. In the parish church she lit a votive candle for her young son who'd recently been mauled in a lion-petting incident.

Arriving belatedly into Tralee, the actress learned that the venue's directors had just emerged from an emergency meeting. They'd issued a terse statement. It said, "Owing to the controversy caused by the visit of Jayne Mansfield, the management of the Mount Brandon Hotel has decided to cancel her appearance."

Mansfield responded with a statement of her own. She said,

"There seems to be a problem. Nobody cancelled my act tonight."
In her version of events, "The musical arrangement for my act
was sent on in advance so that an Irish band could practise it. The
band, I have been told, broke down somewhere and cannot be
located."

The Brandon's dashing manager, Mr. Patrick White, leapt to
the rescue. *Of course* that's what had happened. He'd appreciate it
if everyone could just ignore the original statement which said
the cancellation was due to 'controversy'. "I had the statement
done up and it slipped out by mistake," he pleaded. The Dean of
Kerry presumably didn't buy the missing musicians story. This
was a victory for Christian decency and a personal triumph for
himself and the Bishop. At high mass that evening the Dean
expressed his gratitude to Mr. John Byrne, the hotel's managing
director, for "cancelling this special entertainment".

Jayne Mansfield jetted off for Paris the following day. She'd
netted the hefty sum of £1,000 plus generous expenses for her
flying visit. Even as the star hightailed it out of town, some Tralee
folk were still spoiling for a scrap. The *Irish Press* reported that,
"Tralee residents were considering lodging a protest with RTE over
Saturday night's sketch on 'The Late Late Show' which depicted
three people with placards in protest against Miss Mansfield's visit
in the town. One local resident said, 'This type of thing is not
funny. If RTE want to laugh at Miss Mansfield, alright, but they
should leave the people of Tralee out of it.'"

Rarely has The Point been so consummately missed.

THE MAN IN THE BOOT STOOD UP

The Law Vs. Adam Clayton 1984-89

Adam Clayton was ever the outlaw. Two secondary schools tired of his insolent tomfoolery and bade him a premature farewell. During U2's dogmatic Christian phase his imperviousness to the authority of scripture severely tested the unit's all-for-one, one-for-all ethos. He built a reputation for haircuts which defied convention, not to mention belief.

The law and Adam Clayton came eyeball to eyeball on March 2nd. 1984. The bassist was driving to his Southside home from a wine reception when he happened upon a Garda checkpoint in Harold's Cross. Adam drove blithely on.

Garda Gerald Walsh straddled his motorbike and set off in hot pursuit. Clayton was pulled over. Garda Walsh asked why he hadn't stopped at the checkpoint. "Clayton replied that he was a celebrity in this country and asked how was he to know if they were Gardai or not."

It was a philosophical humdinger worthy of Bishop Berkeley himself. Who can really, *really*, say if a cop is a cop in this illusory world? Unfortunately, Garda Walsh was not in a philosophical frame of mind, especially after Adam told the policeman to "quit messing" and that "he hadn't time to talk". The hole was getting deeper but the star kept digging, insisting "that Garda Walsh would do himself a lot of harm as he (Clayton) was well known high-up".

Point made, Clayton switched on the ignition. The Garda asked him to turn it off. No go. "Garda Walsh told the court that when he leaned in the window to turn off the switch, the car drove off and he was dragged along the road for about 45 feet."

Dusting himself off, the Garda trailed the fugitive musician to his Brighton Square address. Such determined sleuthing did not impress Clayton. "You'll be sorry for this" he told his captor, explaining that "he was the bass player with U2 and he wanted to go home to go to bed". He again asked the Garda to desist from his messing.

Reinforcements arrived to "assist" the musician to Rathmines

Garda Station. It was a contrite Clayton who pleaded guilty to dangerous driving and driving with excess alcohol. Indeed, so impressed was the District Justice with his contriteness that he reduced his driving ban from three years to two. The rising star left the court £225 poorer with the stern caution that he "should be setting an example for the youth of the country".

Four and a half years later Adam Clayton was a megastar. Perhaps his fabulous wealth and fame aroused a twinge of begrudgery in someone less well endowed. In any case, "a complaint" was made which led one Garda Moody to a black Aston Martin in the car park of the Blue Light pub in the Dublin Mountains.

A man was sitting in the open boot of the car, surrounded by others. Garda Moody announced that he was going to search the car for drugs. "On hearing this, the man in the boot stood up and walked away." Adam Clayton should have remembered the lesson of the U2 song: *If you walk away, walk away/I will follow.* Adam walked into a buzzing courtroom on September 1st 1989 to face charges of possession and intent to supply. Nineteen grammes of cannabis resin was a weighty matter.

Justice Windle, presiding, inquired as to how many "cigarettes" the haul amounted to. He was told 150. The judge chuckled and said "Oh, people are allowed to bring 200 cigarettes through customs from Duty Free - but not cannabis." In the public gallery Larry Mullen had to chuckle. Beside him Paul McGuinness didn't. Beside him a little gouger in a Guns 'N' Roses jacket entertained the throng by mimicking the manager's crossed arms and grave expression.

Justice Windle continued to extemporise for no-one in particular. "I don't know anything about these singing groups" he stated in time-honoured judgely fashion, "but I understand that they have some influence on children, youths and - how long do they listen to this stuff? - until they're about thirty I suppose."

So Adam got another lecture about influencing young people. With the state withdrawing the trafficking charge, there remained the possession case. To the astonishment of many - doubtless including several people serving time for drugs offences - Justice

Windle announced that possessing nineteen grammes of cannabis resin was "on a very low scale of importance". Moreover, Adam had been given the drugs as a present, he was of good character, he "bitterly regretted this incident" and he was now going to contribute £25,000 to the Women's Aid Refuge Centre.

Adam had found what he was looking for.

A waiting Mercedes whisked the bassist away to freedom. Ace reporter Liam Fay lingered on the courthouse steps with an old man who'd earlier given Adam a congratulatory slap on the back. "Ah, well, sure he's a great singer," sighed the oul' fella, "A great singer."

A WOMAN FROM DONEGAL SAID THAT SOMEONE STITCHED HER UP

The Chairgate Affair 1997

It started on "The Late Late Show" and finished with the lady vanishing. Siubhan Maloney was the name, restoring antiques was the game. In February 1997 the Donegal woman appeared on "The Late Late Show" with a decrepit bundle of sticks and the decayed remains of a book. Three months on, Siubhan and her fellow contestants returned for the last show of the season. She put the others in the shade. Her pile of firewood had been transformed into a veritable Peacock Throne. Her crock of pages had become an elegant volume fit to adorn the finest drawing room. This was sheer alchemy, the stuff of princes from frogs, dinosaurs from DNA. Siubhan's First Prize was £1,000 worth of Paul Costelloe glassware. It was Friday night.

Sunday, bloody Sunday. Siubhan was in the wars. A Dublin craftsman called Joshua Duffy had told a newspaper that the upholstery on the award-winning chair was his handiwork. He'd webbed the frame, applied hession and sewed in horsehair. Then he'd added wadding, buttoned the leather hide and spent two and a half days attaching 800 studs. He'd also inserted brass inkwells into the arms. Duffy revealed he'd been paid £300 for the work. He'd blown the whistle on Siubhan, he said, because she'd failed to give him due credit on the telly.

According to the rules of the antiques restoration competition, contestants must be amateurs. Professional help was permitted, but the competitors were obliged to declare any assistance to the judges. A contestant's chances of winning would diminish in inverse proportion to the amount of outside help enlisted. Joshua Duffy's claims raised serious questions about the legitimacy of Siubhan's triumph, but things were about to get a lot worse for the "leggy blonde-haired separated mother of two" (© *Sunday World*).

Wednesday morning, and Siubhan and Joshua were at logger-heads on the radio. Pat Kenny refereed the bout. Siubhan let it be known that she was taking legal advice over Joshua's claims. This meant there would be certain issues she couldn't discuss. She could, however, say for certain that the upholsterer "didn't touch" her chair and that she had done "ninety-nine per cent" of the work herself. Joshua, emiting an orchestral gamut of disbelieving noises, said that Siubhan had observed him closely and taken exhaustive notes. Besides, anyone could see that this type of reconstructive surgery was beyond an amateur. "It makes a mockery of our trade," he fumed, "It simplifies a skill which takes years to learn." Siubhan stood her ground. Joshua may indeed have worked on a chair, she said, but not on her chair.

Pat helpfully suggested that the matter could be resolved if Siubhan and Joshua ironed out their differences at a neutral venue, say on his live TV show the coming Saturday. Siubhan could bring along the disputed chair, he said. If only it were that simple. Y'see, the thing was, she'd sold the chair the day after her "Late Late Show" victory, to an anonymous buyer for an undisclosed sum. Still, she said, if the chair's new owner was agreeable, she'd have "no problem with it".

"Joshua?" said Pat.

"Yeah", snorted Joshua, his delivery of searing disgust note-perfect. "Yeah," he said, "So the chair's going to go missing now. It's sold. And the person won't be able to bring it back. It's a total con job, Pat. She's in a hole and now she's digging a bigger hole for herself. If she admitted that I had done the chair it would be a seven day wonder. People would forget about this in a few weeks' time, but now she's diggin', diggin', diggin'…"

Siubhan dug in: "I can't accept that Joshua. I can't admit that you did a chair for me that you had nothing to do with. You said that I should have given you a plug. How could I give you a plug when you had nothing to do with my chair."

At this, Joshua sprang his secret weapon. "Pat," he said, "I can prove that that chair… If she can bring that chair onto the show I can prove that. Now, I'm not telling her how I can prove it, but I can."

"Okay," said Pat, translating for the listeners, "There's something you know about the chair that you did, and you would be able to definitely predict that thing. And we would go look for it. And that would prove that you'd done it."

Joshua pressed home his advantage: "I could strip some of that chair back on the show if you like, and I'll upholster that chair afterwards back to where it was. But I could show you something in that chair. And also something else. I've two things."

Siubhan pounced. "Which means that you set me up from day one!"

"Oh sure," snapped Joshua. "You're saying that I didn't know you."

"No, no, I never said that," Siubhan audibly recoiled. "I said that I met you sometime in March, but that I couldn't put a date on it."

At this point, Kenny stepped in to separate the duellists. He explained to Siubhan that Joshua couldn't possibly have set her up if, as she claimed, he'd never laid a finger on her seat. The radio encounter ended with Joshua, a clear victor on points, spoiling for a televised rematch. Saturday night. No holds barred. Be there.

Siubhan's fighting performance rebounded, producing severe colateral damage. Within hours of her radio appearance, Gerry Kenny of Kenny's Bookbinders announced that he had carried out "ninety-eight per cent" of the work on her antique book. Kenny said that Siubhan had taken "a keen interest" in his methods of restoration but her input was minimal. "She did some finishing," he revealed, "but very little of it because she'd make a mess of it." After that, the deluge.

A company called Traditional Antiques Restoration revealed that they'd fitted the bookstand and worked on the candle-holder. They said they'd come forward because of Siubhan's hint of legal action against Duffy. The firm of RJ Mooney claimed they'd sold Siubhan a whole cow hide at a reduced rate of £100, in return for a mention on "The Late Late Show". Spectrum Tooling said that they'd fitted castors to the chair at a cost of £400, and not £200 as she'd claimed on the television. Longford Brassware Limited and a Galway carpenter had also made substantial contributions to Siubhan's winning effort, taking the final tally of outside agencies to seven.

Saturday morning arrived. Siubhan's antiques antics topped the agenda for Joe Duffy's radio review of the week. "A woman from Donegal said someone had stitched her up," quipped Joe, "I thought she'd done all the work herself." There would be no moment of truth on that night's "Kenny Live" show. Siubhan had gone to ground. Tabloid reporters scoured the West of Ireland for the elusive "forty-year-old beauty". They tracked down Siubhan's boyfriend's wife who sent them packing with the message, "I'm fed up hearing about this bloody chair." They set up sundry stake-outs. One report complained, "there was no sign of Siubhan at one of the country's most idyllic beauty spots."

In the absence of the "blonde beauty" herself, the *Sunday World* trawled Siubhan's past in search of possible answers to the question - Why? The paper revealed its specious findings under the headline "BEAUTY WHO LOVES LIMELIGHT". Siubhan, it reported, was known to have once made a phone call to radio's "Liveline" programme. There was more: "Pictures of Siubhan have also appeared regularly in her local newspaper, the Donegal Democrat." Indeed, just the previous month she had been "starring" in the provincial weekly promoting her aromatherapy business.

The report traced Siubhan's infatuation with fame back twenty-one years. As a teenager, she was placed a creditable third in the Mary From Dungloe beauty pageant. With eye-witness clarity, the *World* recalled, "It was one of her proudest moments. As a delighted Siubhan was showered with huge bouquets of flowers, she could barely control her excitement. She smiled broadly for photographers' cameras and was on top of the world. Siubhan was singled out for special praise for her attitude to the competition, spontaneity and sense of humour. She was just nineteen at the time and relished the attention and publicity."

Siubhan Maloney could have no complaints, the hot seat in which she found herself was entirely of her own making.

A FAIRLY AVERAGE REPUTATION FOR RELIGIOUS TOLERANCE

Ireland Inc. Vs. The Jehovah's Witnesses 1956

Stephen Miller and Henry Bond were just going about their daily business as Jehovah's Witnesses, knocking on doors and asking if people had heard about the One True God. Unfortunately for Miller and Bond, they were in the wrong place at the wrong time to be trying on that sort of thing.

The Witnesses were at the point of knocking off work on Sunday, May 13th 1956. They'd spent a passable afternoon doorstepping the householders of Clonlara, a small townland in County Clare. They'd been well received. Quite a number of people had heard them out. Nobody had slammed the door or fetched out the shotgun.

The pair clambered astride Miller's motorcycle and set off for home, but as they hit the road a car suddenly pulled up in front of them, blocking the way. A group of men began closing in on the motorcycle evangelists. Sensing trouble, Miller scrambled the motorbike over a grass margin in a bid to escape. One of the encroaching men grabbed at Bond's arm, nearly yanking him to the ground.

The Witnesses drove the short distance to an establishment called The Angler's Rest. They needed to use the phone. They were told there was none. Caught in a dead end, there was nothing for it but to face the approaching mob. At the head of the gang was Patrick Ryan, the parish priest. "Are you the men going around distributing and selling heretic books and articles?" he asked, not particularly looking for an answer. The Witnesses were relieved of their bags and briefcases. Miller demanded that the guards be called. The priest replied that no guards were needed to deal with him.

One of the parishioners brandished Miller's vacuum flask and asked the priest if he should break it. He was told not to. Another man thought it would be appropriate to punch Miller on the chin. This was the signal for the mob to give the strangers a good roughing up. The visitors' books and pamphlets were ceremonially burned in the street and the pair were sent packing with a stern warning never to set foot in Clonlara again.

Miller and Bond weren't found wanting for the courage of their convictions. Two months after the Clonlara showdown, Limerick District Court was packed to the rafters for the rematch. Fr. Ryan and ten accomplices were charged with assault and malicious damage. The Bishop of Killaloe, Dr. Rogers, arrived to lend his support from the public gallery. It was reported that "The crowded courtroom rose to their feet as His Lordship entered." The Bishop had made a submission letting the judge know that he stood foursquare behind his curate. Counsel for the defence began by producing a Jehovah's Witness text entitled "Let God Be True". A passage from the book was read out. It stated that the doctrine of the Blessed Trinity was of pagan origin and that Satan was its author. Miller told the court that this was so.

It was pointed out to Miller that he was seeking legal redress under the Constitution of the Republic of Ireland. Did he realise that the self same Constitution commenced with the words, "In the Name of the Most Holy Trinity, from Whom is all Authority"? He replied that he did. The defence put it to Miller that he was of the view that "the laws of the land and the Constitution of this country are under the authority and authorship of Satan, the Devil himself." Miller replied, "It is not surprising when you see the conduct of its ministers of religion." He was in a hole and taking digs.

The defence turned to the conduct of Pastor Russell, the founder of the Jehovah's Witness movement. Was it not true that Russell's wife had accused him of infidelity? Miller replied that he didn't see what this had to do with a mob beating him up at Clonlara.

Henry Bond then told the court that the pair had spent a few hours in Clonlara, giving away books to people who either wouldn't or couldn't pay for them. He told how, at the Angler's Rest, a group of men had seized their bags and burned them. He agreed that the men might have taken exception to a remark of Miller's to the priest. Miller had said "Look here chappie". Perhaps this form of address didn't extend due respect to a parish priest at the head of a belligerent mob.

Bond told the court that he had been raised a Catholic but had been a Jehovah's Witness for the past three years. Hearing this, counsel for the defence told him: "I cannot but feel sorry for you, and I will not cross-examine you." Bond replied that he was "honoured" to have become a Witness and reminded the court that the issue at hand was an "unwarranted" attack on himself and Miller. Margaret O'Donoghue of The Angler's Rest testified to seeing a barracking mob surround the two men. She'd heard one man give the warning: "Do not say 'my dear fellow' to the priest. Address him in the proper manner."

A Garda sergeant said that he'd called to Fr. Ryan's house shortly after the incident. The priest had bluntly informed him that the Jehovah's Witnesses would not be allowed to distribute their literature. Witnesses had been expelled from the parish the previous year and he had instructed his parishioners that if any returned he was to be told straight away.

Counsel for the mob rested his defence on the incontrovertible fact that blasphemy was a crime punishable by statute under the Irish Constitution. He branded Miller "an unusual and an unholy and an unprecedented witness in the witness box, who sees nothing wrong and does not feel in error in telling your worship that Satan himself discovered the doctrine of the Blessed Trinity and therefore commits blasphemy against God and His Blessed Mother." The defence cited a directive in the Constitution ordaining that public homage was due to Almighty God. Furthermore, the defence argued, "This witness is prepared to dishonour the Christian religion, making no distinction between Catholics and non-Catholics." This was a black mark in a country where Catholics and non-Catholics had fought relentlessly for the exclusive franchise on honouring the Christian religion.

Before delivering his verdict, Justice Hurley stressed that the courts were obliged to be non-sectarian. But... "We have," he contended, "a fairly average reputation for religious tolerance in this country, but is religious tolerance to be extended to accept the gospel which Mr. Miller and his companions were disseminating?... The Irish faith is something that has been tempered by the fires of history. It is a tradition, a legend, a way of life. It has its roots in lovely villages and mountains, in prison cells and on the scaffold, and in sorrowful mother's hearts."

Miller and his fellow-travellers sought to destroy that picture-box religion, said the judge. They were guilty of blasphemy in the Catholic understanding of the word. In this light, even though the charge of assault was proven, he would dismiss it under the Probation of Offenders Act. As for the other charges against the mob, he'd dismiss them too.

The judge didn't want any repetition of this case. As a preventative measure he bound both Miller and Bond over to the peace on massive sureties of £200 each. He warned that if they were involved in any more incidents they'd go to prison for three months. The Witnesses' solicitor asked the judge to fix recognizances in case of an appeal. The judge rebuked him: "Sit down, you have no standing in this court." The solicitor informed the judge that, "your worship's decision is unprecedented and contrary to the law of the country. I say that without fear of contradiction." He was wasting his breath.

There was no public outcry over this glaring piece of rough justice. Possession was nine-tenths of the law, and a judge, a Bishop and a priest possessed enough pooled clout to write their own rules. Only the *Irish Times* raised the civil libertarian angle, and that paper's leader writer was careful to express an appropriate level of disdain for the ill-served religious weirdoes. The editorial stated, "The consequence seems to be that people going peacefully about their work not merely can have their property seized and destroyed, but need not consider themselves entitled to the protection of the law."

It stressed, "We know little about the particular tenets of the Jehovah's Witness, and that little we dislike. Nevertheless, these men have the same right as any other religious sect, whether Christian, Jewish, Mahommedan, Taoist or Hindu, to propagate their faith by peaceful means. Any denial of that right is a reflection of the state of freedom in this country. Most Irishmen feel a sense of outrage when a Christian priest is prohibited from pursuing his sacred mission in communist countries; yet what so often and so deplorably happens there has been re-enacted in County Clare and endorsed in Limerick."

But if the *Irish Times* was the conscience of trendy liberalism in Ireland, its time had yet to come. A simple truth prevailed - God was a Catholic. And so long as that remained the case Jehovah's Witnesses and their ilk would be unwelcome interlopers, at large in the State with no invisible means of support.

THE PRAISE OF CERTAIN ELECTRICAL GOODS

Mike Murphy Vs. Colm Tobin 1985-96

Mike Murphy is not one to bear grudges. But the patron saint of Ireland's card scratchers was willing to make an exception for Colm Tobin. Murphy's 1996 autobiography cast Tobin, the "fairly successful author", as an "archetypal school sneak" and a coward to boot. It all began *fadó fadó*...

The bad blood concerned a radio column which appeared in *Magill* magazine early in 1985. The subject was Mike Murphy. The teasing title was "A Little Knowledge Is A Dangerous Thing". The by-line credited one Donal Whelan, a nomme de guerre of the type widely employed to camouflage snipers who might otherwise never eat lunch in this town again. Colm Tobin was that soldier.

The premise of the piece was simple: Mike used to be the High King of light entertainment, but he mislaid his crown when he got his head stuck up his arts. According to the article, the rot set in when Mike fell under the influence of an erudite radio producer, Gene Martin. Consequently, "Young Murphy was... dragged around auction rooms and forced to look at pictures. He developed an interest in pictures". Tobin chronicled how Mike established himself as "a regular feature of art openings", eventually becoming a leading light of the canvas and canapé set.

This metamorphosis irked the radio critic, who scoffed that "during the opening of Gwen O'Dowd's first show at the Project Mr. Murphy turned to the person beside him and muttered: 'Very reminiscent of Barrie Cooke'. But the fact that the paintings weren't even slightly like Barrie Cooke's didn't dampen Mr. Murphy's enthusiasm for art. He began to open shows himself."

There was worse still. "The problem was that Mike started to interview artists the odd morning. His voice changed, he began to talk through his nose; he tried to sound knowledgeable... It was awful. One morning he had a woman called Anne Crookshank, who is some sort of art historian, on. She mentioned an obscure painting by an old master. She asked Mike if he knew it. No, he said he didn't. Ms Crookshank continued talking. Suddenly, Mike began to interrupt her, yes, yes, actually, he did know the painting. He had just remembered." *Ow!*

The charge sheet lengthened. "The interviews with artists got worse and worse... As time went by the questions grew longer, statelier and more pretentious. The people of Ireland were suffering hugely." Apparently, a novelist was approached to go on the show. He declined. "The researcher said that Mike had gone to a lot of trouble. What sort of trouble, asked the novelist. Well, he's read one of your books. Expletive deleted, said the novelist. Mike was starting to read." *Ouch!*

And so to the diagnosis. Mike had "caught something from art". Transplanted from his natural environment, his easy chirpiness had given way to "embarrassment", "nerviness" and "angst". The erstwhile light banter-weight champ was all psyched-out from "looking at paintings and reading books. When he sits in the studio he carries the burden of all these things with him. He wants to be serious and enlightening and it is awful to watch him try."

The final blow of the hatchet was an imagined scenario which anticipated by five years Murphy's "Scrap Saturday" caricature. Mike is interviewing the artist Sidney Nolan, going at it "straight from the nose". Mike: "Sidney Nolan, you... you have been well known... you... you are an artist, a painter, someone whose name is known... you... you have been all over the world... critics have described your work... your work has been highly praised."

Bullseye. But there was a telling disparity in tone between Tobin's withering *Magill* demolition and Dermot Morgan's subsequent lampoon (Mike singing the praises of a fire extinguisher hanging on a gallery wall etc.). In the light of "Scrap Saturday"'s sharp but affectionate joshing, Tobin's piece resembled a callous mugging. A decade later, committing his memoirs to print, Mike was still smarting. His words bristled on the page. Tobin's attack, he wrote, "dealt viciously, savagely and insultingly with my professional life and personality".

The vast majority of people who aren't Mike Murphy might conclude that Tobin's real transgression was to fall foul of a zealot's lack of perspective. While the "Scrap Saturday" crew were rowdy rapscallions on a turkey-shoot, he was a warrior-pilgrim on a solemn crusade. He and his fellows at *Magill* - Gene Kerrigan, John Waters, Michael Dwyer, Olivia O'Leary, Fintan O'Toole, Mark Brennock *et al* - were the brightest and best in the land. They fought tooth and nail to put transparency, accountability and liberalism on the agenda of Irish public life. They met resistance at every turn.

Viewed from inside the bunker, *Magill* was a Galapagos of cultural giantism rising above a slithery sea of political sleveenism and anti-enlightenment gombeenism. And keepers of the flame tend to get tetchy when they're asked to shove over and make way for a non-initiate, especially someone "who devotes a lot of time to the praise of certain electrical goods" (a reference to the popular TV show "Murphy's Micro Quiz-M"). So Colm used a megaton of napalm to cook Murphy's goose when a good basting at Gas Mark 5 would have left a better taste.

Mike was "astounded by the savagery of the attack". He was even more astounded when a colleague subsequently revealed the true identity of its author. In the weeks following the article's publication, Tobin had been a regular studio guest of Mike's. Never again. Ever.

Some time later Mike espied Colm attending a play. Mike's dudgeon was stratospheric. He told Colm he was "a craven hypocrite" and "a worthless individual of no principle".

History does not record Tobin's reply.

THEY'LL GO WILD FOR THIS IN AMERICA

Lord Nelson's Downfall 1966

Dubliners had long been embroiled in a love-hate relationship with Nelson's Pillar. The monument had dominated the capital's main artery since 1809. It was known as the "city sofa" because idle citizens would lounge on its steps watching the world go by. The balustrade at the summit afforded an unparalleled view of the capital for just 6d. It was a popular point of departure amongst exhibitionist suicides.

The Pillar was the enemy within. Yeats condemned it as "a monstrosity". Every few years its demolition was debated at official level. In 1891 Dublin's Lord Mayor introduced a removal bill in the Westminster parliament. Dublin Corporation opposed the motion on the grounds of expense. When they discovered that the pillar's trustees would have to bear the cost they did an abrupt u-turn. The outcome of the vote was another stay of execution for Nelson.

The Pillar saw out the Easter Rising, the War Of Independence and the Civil War with barely a scratch. It survived periodic bouts of enthusiasm amongst Dublin Corporation officials for blowing up imperial monuments. In 1929, for instance, King William was blasted from his plinth on College Green. In 1936 the city fathers marked the coronation of George VI by dynamiting his ancestor, George II, on Stephen's Green.

At 1.30am on 8th March 1966 Nelson crashed to earth with a bang. Suspicion fell on the recently dormant IRA. The usual suspects were rounded up and taken to the Bridewell. They were quickly released without charge. The Irish Republican Publicity Bureau issued an immediate denial of any IRA involvement. News of Nelson's downfall elicited an ambivalent mix of amusement, celebration and half-hearted condemnation. The *Irish Times* spoke to an architect surveying the debris. "J. A. Culliton thought it tragic," said the report, "He seemed to be the only one who did."

A Garda spokesman approvingly described the demolition as "a thorough job". The Gardai speculated that the bomb may have detonated prematurely. Anxious to give the bombers the benefit of the doubt, a Garda spokesman expressed the view that it had probably been timed to go off "two or three hours later when there would be less danger of anyone being injured".

The device exploded upwards and outwards causing minimal colateral damage. One Garda on the scene grinned broadly as he described it as, "an absolutely perfect job. Not a window broken in the Post Office. Perfect." Another Garda reflected gleefully, "They will go wild about this in America!"

The country was abuzz with preparations for the Golden Jubilee of the Easter Rising. Nobody could be seen to mourn the passing of the imperialist Sea Lord. Dublin's Lord Mayor, Alderman Eugene Timmons, focused his condemnation on the unofficial nature of the demolition, saying "No small group had the right to assume a responsibility which should have been the decision of the local community". An ancestor of the fallen hero took the news graciously. The Honourable George Nelson said, "I am sure there was nothing personal in it."

A street carnival broke out around the scene of the explosion. A huge crowd of sightseers gathered for a gawk, their numbers swelled by an influx of country folk freed to travel because it was early closing day in rural Ireland. Foolhardy revellers played a game of dare, jinking through the police cordon to pose under the most unstable part of the stump. One report noted: "The young Gardai were harassed and maddened by grown men who found the barrier as great a challenge as the children, and there were some fine displays of running and tackling which brought rousing cheers and jeers from the assembled thousands."

An unidentified man wrapped Nelson's sword in his overcoat and drove off with it. According to one report, "there were happy, smiling faces everywhere and witticisms like 'poor old Nelson' were greeted with roars of laughter." The bombing caught the imagination of the whole country. Within hours of the explosion, punters were flocking into a Ballina pub - 160 miles away - to see a display of Nelson debris put on exhibition by scavenging lorry drivers.

The only moaners were the staff of a store in O'Connell Street which was behind the Garda cordon and therefore devoid of custom.

The mendacious manager refused to give them the day off. Also hit were O'Connell Street's "Nile-siders", the group of families who had for generations passed down the "privilege" of selling fruit and flowers under the shadow of the pillar. The erstwhile statue had commemorated Nelson's victory at the Nile.

When the dust settled, the Lemass government was caught in an embarrassing half-Nelson. Justice Minister Lenihan's description of the event as "reckless" and "an outrage" was dismissed as "tepid" in an *Irish Times* leader. The newspaper summed up the administration's Catch 22 situation, explaining: "The Government is in a sad case. What sort of celebration will it be if they catch the dynamiters and clap them in prison?"

There was no getting away from the Easter Rising and the tide of nationalist triumphalism sweeping the land. Telefís Eireann's newest documentary series was devoted to recalling the great battles against the English. The country's best selling records included a collection of rebel songs by Arthur Murphy and a compilation entitled "From 1916: The Best Of Ireland's Music" featuring such splendours as "Wrap The Green Flag Around Me Boys", "Amhrann Na bFiann" and Pearse's poem, "The Mother".

But 1916 fever wasn't all beer and bunting. For the majority in the North the celebrations commemorated an act of treachery. 1916-mania in the South inevitably portrayed the Six Counties as a spot of unfinished business rather than a legitimate political entity. The Pillar bomb turned up the heat in Northern Ireland. Ian Paisley had already been sowing fears that the Taoiseach's recent ice-breaking visit to Belfast signalled a Stormont sell-out. A few days before the Nelson explosion, the British Military Attaché's home in Dublin had been petrol-bombed. When the Admiral tumbled from his perch, RUC stations across the North were sandbagged in readiness. Austin Currie, the nationalist MP for East Tyrone, received a threatening letter. It informed him he'd be shot if there were any "rebel celebrations of the murders of 1916" in the county.

The cabinet was in a pickle. The St. Patrick's Day parade was one week away. It would be followed shortly by a huge march down O'Connell Street on Easter Sunday which would form the centrepiece of the 1916 commemorations. Members of the Old IRA were to provide the Guard Of Honour. It now seemed likely that they'd be filing past a pile of rubble - an awkward reminder that the aspirations of 1916 remained unfulfilled. Something would have to be done. Three days after the bombing, the Government Information Bureau announced that the remainder of the Pillar would be demolished.

Six days after the first explosion, the Army Bomb Squad completed the job begun by enemies of the state. In a flurry of last minute activity, members of The Royal Institute Of Architects had been denied a High Court injunction against the demolition. The unique Regency lettering at the base of the pillar was sacrificed to political expediency. As *Build* magazine saw it, "The savages have triumphed... the deliberate act of destruction of Thomas Johnston's doric column has been encompassed by unknown elements and the government." The army destroyed the stump in a controlled midnight explosion. Huge crowds gathered to watch and cheer. Radio Eireann captured the whoops and applause so the whole country could share in the fun the next morning.

Unfortunately the controlled explosion didn't live up to its name and, unlike the seditionaries, the army succeeded in wreaking wholesale damage to surrounding buildings, including the General Post Office. As the crowds surged forward for souvenirs, Gardai were deployed to prevent mass pillaging from shattered shopfronts. When St. Patrick's Day arrived, Official Ireland closed ranks on the touchy subject of the Pillar. Television and newspaper pictures of the Dublin parade were angled to omit the tarpaulined scar at the heart of O'Connell Street.

Over the following weeks, visitors flocked into the country to bask in the carnival spirit. Greasy tills rang ceaselessly as the 1916 industry slipped into top gear. Books about the Rising rolled off the presses. Nearly a million commemorative ten shilling coins bearing Pearse's profile entered circulation - via the Royal Mint in London. Eager philatelists flooded the GPO to buy up special edition stamps. CIE's fleet of tardy double-deckers displayed the Sword Of Light, the official 1916 symbol.

Newspapers strained to outdo each other in the scale and

lavishness of their 1916 pull-out supplements. The fervour even spread to perfidious Albion where *The Telegraph* serialised the Rising exploits of De Valera and *The People* cashed in with a pictorial tribute entitled "SIX DAYS TO DEATH". Sticklers for detail complained that the British troops featured in the *People*'s 1916 souvenir publication were actually Irish Free State soldiers fighting in the Civil War of 1921-22. And that the photo of the Four Courts was actually of the Custom House. And that one shot - captioned "A rebel leader brandishes a revolver as he cries 'To your positions!'" - was actually from a Michael Collins election rally of 1922.

As Easter Week approached, Kilkee Town Commission patriotically passed a proposal to enact all its business in Irish. One member stormed out, protesting "I don't know a damn thing you are talking about". He wasn't the only one. The inaugural meeting as gaeilge lasted precisely twenty-one minutes instead of the usual two hours.

Croke Park was the venue for a major Easter Week entertainment extravaganza to commemorate The Rising. Seating was available for 18,000 people nightly. The spectacular pageant, entitled "Aiseiri", was a joint production by the Army and the FCA. One first-night notice conveyed the tone of the event, citing, "the torches, the rockets, the canons spitting fire, the Redcoats biting the dust on all sides".

The infectious mood of good-natured Brit bashing inspired many celebrations of an impromptu nature. Nelson's Archway in Skibbereen was blown up in the dead of night. "UP THE REBELS" was daubed large on Cavan's Protestant Hall. In Dun Laoghaire, well-wishers painted the town green. Amongst an assortment of republican slogans was the scrawl "HITLER WAS A GOOD FELLOW".

By the time the Easter holiday weekend arrived, the Stormont parliament had rushed through several new laws. The North's Home Affairs Minister was empowered to translate the prevailing bunker mentality into physical fact. The Stormont administration effectively closed the border from the Saturday morning to Sunday night by cancelling the North/South train service and manning all crossings. Meanwhile in Dublin, a fair job had been made of expunging Nelson's remains from the scene of the crime. There were other embarrassments, however. The Protestant Archbishop of Dublin, Dr. Simms, found himself locked out of the formal opening of the Garden Of Remembrance. His Grace stood outside for most of the ceremony while red-faced officials searched for a key to admit him.

There was worse. The focal point of the Easter Sunday commemorations was the Presidential viewing stand at the General Post Office. When President De Valera took his place to oversee the Easter Parade, wide open spaces were clearly visible in the VIP seating around him. Comical scenes ensued, as prominent guests were shooed in from the margins to flesh out the President's television backdrop.

And so the most lavish expression of national pride in the history of the young state degenerated into a petty political squabble over invitations. Fine Gael and Labour expressed their disappointment that the Fianna Fail administration had been so small-minded as to snub them. The relevant government department, Defence, issued an apology saying it "sincerely regrets this error". Fianna Fail pointed out that some of its own ministers hadn't been invited, evidence of a genuine mistake. They suspected that the Fine Gael and Labour leaders had deliberately stayed away to generate a row.

Lord Nelson's assailants saved the government further blushes by evading capture.

A TERRIBLE BLUNDER

The American Nightmare Vs. Ben Dunne 1992

It was in the paper so it must be true. It couldn't be, but it was. Ireland's best known recluse had taken a golf trip and landed in the rough. Spectacularly. Comically. Cruelly.

It was a Sunday morning in March 1992 when the three-day-old news broke. Ben Dunne, the publicity-shy Chairman of Dunnes Stores, had been arrested in a Florida hotel. Orlando police had spent sixty-five minutes trying to talk the former *Checkout* magazine "Man Of The Year" off a 17th floor balcony. They were afraid he might jump. He was spooked, wild-eyed. "It was like he was a cornered animal fearful that something was going to kill him," said one witness.

Dunne screamed at those nearest to him to "Get the police!" They were the police. He was surrounded by his own demons. Guests were cleared from the atrium far below, just in case. Dunne was eventually persuaded to step back towards his room. Police officers downed him and slapped on handcuffs. He was wearing just his underpants.

The immediate crisis was over, but the plot thickened. The police uncovered a small amount of cocaine, then a large amount, 32.5 grammes. They also found a lady who was not his wife. Ms. Denise Wojcik (22) identified herself as an employee of the "Escorts In A Flash" agency. Dunne was hospitalised. A police report stated, "He was taken into custody at the hospital and at that point there was a brief struggle." The tycoon was charged with trafficking cocaine. He was released on bail of $25,000.

At the time of Ben Dunne's balcony scene, the Hyatt Regency Grand Cypress hotel was teeming with Irish journalists on a U2 concert junket. The by-line of a lifetime was right under their noses but no-one got a snort. Dunne re-entered Ireland from Britain under an assumed name. Three days after his arrest the story finally caught up with him via a tip-off from the Irish embassy in Washington to a *Sunday Tribune* stringer in New York. The news beggared belief. Could upstanding Doctor Shekels really be crazed Mister Hyde? Ben Dunne had always jealously kept himself to himself. What little the public did know of him suggested a shy, hard-nosed workaholic with a puritanical streak.

Ben wasn't given to fripperies. Once he'd been asked if he'd consider buying a private jet. He answered that he'd rather use the cash to buy another supermarket which would "make more money" for him. He had no time for the glitterati, preferring to sup a quiet pint or two with close friends. The trappings of his vast wealth were few, if you except the tight security cordon around his north Dublin home.

Dunne had always kept a wary distance from the media. One source revealed: "The phone calls which are returned are from the man himself but he never admits it - 'just say it's a spokesman for Dunnes Stores' is the customary response." "He is not a confident public speaker", said another observer. "Ben Dunne will rarely negotiate with unions," reported an IDATU official, adding "When he does, he is not a pretty sight."

Now things had come to a sorry pass for the bluff man of few words. Within hours of his disgrace becoming public, he opted to perform an act of contrition in the full glare of the despised media. Firstly he wanted to stress that suicide had never been in his thoughts. He stated, "The main reason for the panic was that I had taken substances that I shouldn't have." He regarded the matter as "a terrible blunder".

"I can blame no-one only myself," he said. "I am not a cocaine user. In a weak moment I took the goddamn stuff and in no way am I looking for pity. I took it, I shouldn't have taken it. Just in the same way, I am not an alcoholic. I took cocaine and I won't be taking it again."

Having admitted, "It was hard to be arrested as a dealer", the shopping magnate set the record straight on his personal consumption habits. "I am not addicted to any drugs, legal or otherwise," he insisted. "There is an awful lot of prescribed drugs that I wouldn't take. I don't drink shorts. I drink beer. I am not interested in drinking shorts because I am afraid to."

He said the fiasco in Orlando had put his job at risk. In that regard he was no different to any other Dunnes Stores manager. He believed it would be some time before he could expect people to see him "in the right light" again. He explained, "If there was someone like that around me it would take me time before I had confidence enough that these people were stable."

In the heel of the hunt, it had been a learning experience. Things don't go better with coke. He told the nation: "I was not aware of the effects. If I was I would not have taken it. Having said that, I am delighted that what happened has happened because I can say with certainty now that I would not take it again."

It was good to be back in the land of the law-abiding.

A ROW IN THE HOUSE

Damian Corless Vs. "Into The Heart" £12.95

It all began on a bleak morning in early 1981 when middle-aged couple Martin and Kathleen Corless pulled out of their driveway to go to work. After travelling a few yards they joined a line of stalled cars. A bus had come to grief at the end of the icy road.

There were other routes off the estate. Martin flicked the indicator and began to turn the car around. A motorbike speeding down the wrong side of the street braked hard to avoid a collision. Martin rolled down the window to remonstrate with the reckless rider. The term "road-rage" was unknown at the time, but semantics alone couldn't shield Martin from a barrage of hysterical punches.

By teatime Martin was sporting a horrific shiner and cursing the seatbelt that had rendered him a sitting target. The table was being cleared when an excited neighbour rang at the door. Come see, more motor madness! Outside, a car had swerved violently across the oncoming lane and ploughed into a telegraph pole.

Martin and Kathleen joined the knot of concerned neighbours at the scene. In the confusion, nobody paid much heed to the phone cables trailing from the felled mast. These cables, shrouded in dusk, now formed a tripwire across the road. The first passing car sprang the trap.

The car, when it came, snagged the fallen wires and lurched onward like a harpooned whale. High on a nearby gable the wire strained at its bracket. The bracket formed the third point of a triangle completed by the moving car and fallen pole (*see p.344, Fig.1a*). As the cable jerked rigid, it shot the pole into the air. As the pole flew upwards, a steel foothold struck the back of Kathleen's head. The projectile reached its maximum altitude and the cable snapped. The mast fell to Earth, pinning Martin to the ground.

An ambulance whisked the injured couple away. The onlookers' attentions turned to the driver who'd crashed in the first place. He was unscathed. He'd dashed the short distance home to phone the gardai. The kids milling around identified him as Bono out of U2.

My parents survived to tell the tale. I told it to anyone who'd listen. Hard as I looked, though, I could never find a good enough reason to put it in print. It was just a freak incident completely unrelated to U2's soaraway success story. Until the publication of Niall Stokes' 1996 U2 hagiography, "Into The Heart".

In the book, Bono's friend and collaborator Gavin Friday discusses the U2 song "I Threw A Brick Through A Window". As Gavin relates it, "Bono was going to a party with Alison and he decided to splash out on a bottle of wine... There was this couple up the road called Mr. & Mrs. Curley, and Bono was driving this crock of a car - and whatever he did he crashed into Mr. & Mr. Curley's gate and the whole fucking post fell into the garden. The wine spilt all over the car and the Gardai thought he'd been drinking. And there were all these fucking neighbours, all these two-faced Catholics, standing in judgement. And it was, like, 'I have to get out of this fucking kip'. So there was this sort of brick through the window of that Gay Byrne world that was closing in on us all. And the feeling was: Sorry, Cedarwood has to go."

This is surprising. At the time of the accident, sightings of U2 were very rare in the Dublin suburb of Cedarwood. A major British, European and US tour had kept them beyond the gaze of the local window-squinters for most of the previous six months. A long slog around Europe beckoned within days. And spare a thought for Gavin's two-faced Catholic Gaybo-fixated neighbours. Simply clapping eyes on the painted style-terrorist in those days imbued the sensation of being press-ganged onto the judging panel for Alternative Miss World. Easy on the eye he was not.

Back to the book. In the very next paragraph, Bono explains that the song in question was about "a row in the house". End of story. So Gavin's garbled outburst was just a gratuitous car-crash anecdote, a jigsaw piece that didn't fit but was bunged into place anyway. And Niall Stokes let the name Curley pass when he knew full well it was Corless.

Perhaps Niall would argue that these are trifling details, that an impressionistic mish-mash is even better than the real thing. To do so, however, he'd have to apply a different set of standards to those brought to bear by his own magazine on Eamon Dunphy's

"Unforgettable Fire" biography.

"FOUL!" screamed the *Hot Press* headline. Dunphy's tome was gleefully savaged as an "ill-researched" error-riddled "travesty". "The pettiness of each of these errors does not mean they can be simply disregarded," censured the mag. "The truth is that they combine to distort the big picture."

Dunphy's book got Niall's school wrong. This was seized upon by the writer of the critique, Neil McCormack, as evidence of a deeper failing. "In getting his facts wrong," he charged, "Dunphy not only insults the people involved, he throws entirely false light on the picture with a simple fact that, if he was not entirely certain of it, he need never have included in the first place. It suggests a lack of knowledge, a lack of research - and ultimately a lack of care."

Enough said. Oh, except that the nascent U2 first gigged in 1976, not '74 as Niall's book states. And U2 have a song called "Some Days Are Better Than Others". Towards the end of Stokes' exhaustive study - p.119, to be precise - that title is rendered as "Some Songs Are Better Than Others".

Dr. Freud was unavailable for comment.

AN UNPLEASANT DUTY TO CRITICISE FOUL PLAY

Tipperary GAA Vs. The Dublin Media 1968

The earliest known hurling contest took place in 1272 BC. The match report appeared, two millennia later, in the Mediaeval "Book Of Leinster". It makes rousing reading. While the native Fir Bolg and the invading Tuatha De Danann were killing time before the Battle Of Moytura, it was decided to have a 27-a-side limber-up. There was no time limit. Both sides simply hacked at each other "until their bones were broken and bruised and they fell outstretched on the turf and the match ended." In place of the modern lap of honour, the victorious Fir Bolg hurlers fell upon their crippled opponents and slew them.

While the primal bloodlust at the core of most sports has become stylised and diluted out of all recognition, hurling has retained much of its untamed purity. In this cosseted age of dental floss, men's deodorants and brain-scan machines, hurling's deep entanglement with violence has increasingly become the love that dare not speak its name. There was a time, not so long ago, when it was all very different. In 1965, for instance, Mr. M. Costigan didn't feel in the least bit ridiculous telling the Laois GAA County Board: "The (foreign games) Ban should be retained. Men like Davis, Pearse and Wolfe Tone died for its retention." Everyone knew what he meant. Some years later an internal GAA document stressed, "We would like to emphasise that the spirit as well as the letter of our amateur status rules and regulations should be appreciated and honoured by all our units." Fightin' words, and no mistake.

The GAA first started getting sensitive about its violent reputation at the peak of the Sixties' peace'n'love craze. LSD provided the Association with a powerful motivation. They saw they could make big profits by pushing their wares in the schoolyards. The new Hurling Revival Plan was a spectacular success, generating pounds, shillings and pence in abundance. Orders for juvenile hurleys from January to July 1968 were up ten thousand on the same period in 1967. But there was still resistance to the ancient game from modern parents who wanted their little Jimmy to go out into the world with a full set of teeth, ten working fingers and an outward-facing nose.

Anxious parents would not have been reassured by the 1968 National League Hurling Final, a game worthy of that legendary clash between the Fir Bolg and Tuatha De Danann. The combatants were Tipperary and Kilkenny. Recent meetings between the sides had produced several hospitalisations and a catalogue of standing vendettas. Before the Final was very old, the thin line between healthy competition and gang warfare had evaporated in a red mist. "TIPPERARY VICTORS IN GAME OF UGLY INCIDENTS" was the *Irish Times'* verdict. According to that paper, "The needle which has marred a number of recent matches between these counties again thrust up its ugly and malicious spike."

The first outbreak of extra-curricular violence came when Tipperary's Len Gaynor was felled by a blow on the head. "A short fracas ensued." Moments later, the hapless Gaynor was whacked by a spectator as he shimmied down the touchline. Shortly afterwards there was an off-the-ball incident in the Kilkenny goal-mouth. Kilkenny goalkeeper Ollie Walsh "was laid prostrate by a blow from behind." The match official had no sympathy for the poleaxed goalie. "As Walsh lay on the ground the referee ordered Jimmy Doyle of Tipperary to proceed to play the ball." This, felt the reporter, was "the limit of absurdity". Failing to take advantage of the goalkeeper's horizontal posture, Doyle put his shot over the bar for a point. "Had he scored a goal, a riot could have developed."

The following week, the GAA's Central Council convened at their Croke Park headquarters to review the carnage. The Association's President, Mr. F. Muldoon, took pains to point out that - leaving aside the assault, fracas, spectator ambush, attack and counter-attack - the game was mostly played as the GAA would like all games to be played. Michael Maher of the Tipperary County Board thought that the press had a case to answer. By drawing attention to the violence, the newspapers had passed up a golden opportunity to emphasise the sportsmanship on view. The Kilkenny Board Chairman, Nicky Purcell, didn't see what all the fuss was about. "I am not being glib," he said, "when I say that this was not the first time, nor will it be the last time that these things will happen." Purcell, too, felt let down by the press. "I wonder have they harped on it too much," he mused.

Six weeks later, the GAA's Central Council announced its verdict. Tipperary's John Flanagan and Kilkenny's Ollie Walsh were meted out six-month suspensions. Walsh denied that he'd provoked Flanagan by giving him a good clatter. His protests were in vain. The Tipperary County Board fingered the blame for the suspensions firmly on the press. The newspapers had "created a climate of public opinion" which had forced the Central Council down this appalling vista.

"JUST WHO DID THE PRESS STRIKE?" shrieked one of the shot messengers, in this case the *Irish Independent*. The newspaper expressed "sorrow" that a "responsible" body of men could make a statement so "utterly untenable, and some of which displays an astonishing lack of knowledge of, or disregard for, the rules of hurling." The *Independent* threw the rulebook at Tipperary. Rule 96 clearly stated that, "A player deliberately striking an opponent or deliberately kicking him shall incur suspension for not less than six months." So there.

Ollie Walsh appealed against the severity of the ban. His county Chairman, Nicky Purcell, came to his defence. The suspension should be reduced, Purcell stated. A main plank of his argument was that the people of Kilkenny were against it. He got no joy. Nicky Purcell was furious. He wanted to know, "why was not last year's All-Ireland Hurling Final between the two teams investigated? During it, one Kilkenny player lost an eye, another recieved multiple fractures to his wrist, another finished the game with concussion and a fourth had an index finger broken." And now, suddenly, players were to be held accountable to the rulebook. Three thousand years of tradition was being turned on its head.

All of a sudden, it seemed, fair was foul and foul was unfair. Michael Maher of Tipperary blamed the press for tampering with the climate. At this point, though, the GAA's Central Council was determined to blow full-time on the matter. All appeal routes were closed off. Tipperary's only sensible option now was to knuckle down and concentrate on the impending All-Ireland

Championship. Instead, the county launched a surprise unilateral offensive. The Tipperary Board slapped a ban on six named journalists who'd penned blow-by-blow accounts of the rumble with Kilkenny. The Dublin-based newspapers were to be starved of the lifeblood of Tipperary GAA affairs.

The *Irish Independent*'s GAA correspondent responded: "It pains me grievously that a group of mature men… should act like a spoiled, only child festering with an imaginary grievance." The writer wanted the GAA Central Council to suspend Tipperary for bringing the game into disrepute. Weeks passed. The Dublin chapel of the National Union of Journalists finally retaliated on August 25th 1968, instructing its members not to handle any Tipperary GAA news. The Tipperary board picked that same day to announce the lifting of its ban. The county said it would re-instate normal relations with the NUJ from the following Wednesday, four days before Tipperary were to meet Wexford in the 1968 All-Ireland Hurling Final.

If only it were that simple. The national press was going to make Tipperary pay. In the run-up to the All-Ireland Final, the Wexford team's build-up was given blanket coverage, with daily reports and individual player profiles. Tipperary were mentioned strictly in passing. The big game produced a shock. There was more than a hint of glee in headlines like "WEXFORD TORPEDO TIPPERARY" which greeted the underdogs' triumph. The vanquished Tipperary players repaired to the Spa Hotel in Lucan to bathe their wounds. There, the General Secretary of the GAA made a special point of praising their conduct on the pitch that day. The Bishop of Clonfert added that the Tipperary Board were perfectly entitled to resent any outside criticism they liked.

It was the end of the Championship line for Tipperary, but not for the anti-Dublin resentment they'd articulated and embodied. In a wildcat strike, Derry's GAA Board notified the NUJ that the county would be imposing a news ban on the Republic's national newspapers. Cork were next to air festering grievances. Three days after losing the 1968 Minor Hurling Final to Wexford, the Cork Board attacked the Dublin newspapers for pinning nasty "incidents" on their minors. Cork selector Frank Murphy complained: "The reports are typical of those of the past four All-Ireland Finals, when lavish praise was given to Wexford and little to Cork."

The press had reported Cork's rough stuff, Murphy complained, but they'd made no mention of the Wexford man booked for using his hurley as an offensive weapon, or of the vicious assault on Cork's goalkeeper as he lay injured. Murphy wanted it known that one of the Cork players criticised for violence had himself suffered a gash in the head that needed five stitches. And as for the Wexford Minor carried off the pitch, Cork Chairman Jack Barrett believed that the use of a stretcher had been "unnecessary".

Cork's criticism stung the *Independent*'s Mitchel Cogley into a bizarre rebuff. He wrote: "Where minors are concerned, it is an unpleasant duty - but a duty, nevertheless - to have to criticise foul play." Press relations with Tipperary reached a new low when the Dublin branch of the NUJ extended its ban to include any written or photographic evidence of GAA activity in the county, from Senior matches to pub raffles.

Wexford were next to take a swing at the press. Apparently, the routine mayhem of a hurling final in Enniscorthy had been blown out of all proportion by reporters who seemed to have an unhealthy fascination with gore. One member of the County Board objected that, "A lot of commendable things happen in County Wexford that do not get half enough publicity. It is not good enough." His colleague, Mr. Doran, was concerned about Wexford's image abroad. "I know people who read that report in America," he said. Mr. P. Codd complained, "It was stated that one man was kicked in the face on the ground, and everyone here knows that is not true." The Chairman, Sean Browne, felt honour-bound to point out that it *was* actually true. The referee had noted the incident in graphic detail in his match report. Still, the weight of opinion on the Wexford Board was that the press had let the sport down yet again.

In Christmas week 1968 the NUJ lifted its embargo on Tipperary as a gesture of goodwill and reconciliation. The bloodshed continues.

THE FAMILY TRIED TO STOP HIM WATCHING

The League Of Decency Vs. "The Spike" 1978

It was yet another cowardly capitulation on the part of the national broadcaster but, for once, the Dublin 4 set and the Backwoods Brigade found themselves in full agreement - the sudden demise of "The Spike" had been a mercy killing. The school-based drama series had taken Irish television down corridors which must be bricked off forever.

It was early 1978 when RTE took a much hyped plunge into gritty contemporary drama. Scripted by a forty-year-old teacher, Patrick Gilligan, "The Spike" was trumpeted as a warts'n'all examination of urban life as it manifested itself in a Dublin technical school.

The first few episodes passed by uneventfully enough - there were some complaints about crude language, but nothing to fuse the switchboards. On the contrary, the viewing public warmed to the series in sufficient numbers to put the show at No. 3 in the TAM ratings behind perennial favourites "Hall's Pictorial Weekly" and "Quicksilver".

The critics, however, were damning of this mutant offspring of "Please Sir!" and "Colditz". "The Spike", they concurred, was fabulously bad. One writer reflected disdainfully that it was "ill-judged, badly-written, wildly exaggerated, tasteless, naive and so embarrassing in its infantile approach to serious matters." Another described the early episodes as "hamfisted, lurid melodrama." In addition, several teachers groups tut-tutted that their profession was being called into disrepute.

They had a point. In one bedroom scene the school's pensive headmaster is asked by his wife what he's thinking about. "Hoors," he replies. By Episode 4 there were mutterings that the show was calling the acting profession into disrepute. In this instalment the principal's daughter enrolls in The Spike as a last resort, having been expelled from her convent school. The young girl isn't settled in a wet day when one of the teachers plies her with gin in an effort to have his wicked way with her. The attempted seduction traumatises an eavesdropping associate. And so the corridors of a tough Dublin comprehensive resonate with the poesy of dementia: "Light came from my fingernails. Deep in honeyed flesh sweet buds catch fire... Birthwards there is such pain, such pangs, such joy." Such utter crap had seldom been witnessed in the history of Irish television.

"The Spike" had come off its hinges. *Hibernia* magazine's television critic could only applaud. "I vowed a couple of weeks ago that I would write nothing more on this blackboard bungle,' he wrote, "but the series is now becoming cherishable... RTE seems to have found the magic formula for successful comedy." Others were not so amused. The knives were out for "The Spike", but nobody could quite believe it when the intended victim gleefully impaled itself in a pre-meditated act of hari-kiri. It was Episode 5. The plot of that landmark instalment is worth recounting.

The school is hosting a series of evening classes in subjects which include Fur Appreciation, Overcoming Shyness and Floor Scrubbing (I jest not). In a not untypical line of dialogue, the Fur Appreciation teacher advises, "Having got your skin soft and pliable you will be ready for formication." *Fwoooarr*, missus! Meanwhile, the teacher giving the class in Overcoming Shyness is so painfully bashful that he tanks up beforehand on Dutch courage. This paves the way for a hilarious scenario where the emboldened pedant demonstrates the techniques of "bottom pinching" and "the friendly crotch grab". The episode reaches its surreal climax when the shyest girl in the class is miraculously cured. Quick as a flash she's next door whipping off her kit for the still life art group, and the viewing nation.

Strange but true: sown into the fabric of Episode 5 was an off-hand disparaging reference by one of the teachers to the "League Of Decency". Slump forward Mr. J. B. Murray, founder and Chairman of an organization by the same name. Sitting at home that evening maintaining his customary vigil against filth, Mr. Murray was seized with apoplexy. His wife told the press, "He got a pain in his chest while telephoning the newspapers to complain." According to the *Irish Times* , "The family tried to stop him watching it... but he insisted and he got very worked up by the nude scene."

Meanwhile, back in the real world, even the most fervent champions of freedom of expression were making heavy going of defending the indefensible. The show's series producer, Noel O'Brien, discharged a round into his own foot by arguing that the programme "was trying to examine attitudes of pupils and staff in a school to nudity".

The countdown to Episode Six was underway and RTE's Director General, Oliver Moloney, had a crisis on his hands. J. B. Murray was on the mend and spoiling for a fight. Several Limerick County Councillors were up in arms and Fine Gael's Education spokesman, Eddie Collins, had drafted a stiff letter. Clearly there was no alternative - Moloney "deferred" the show just hours before the next instalment was due to screen.

"THE SPIKE GETS AXED" proclaimed the *Evening Press* from its front page, although the shock news hadn't reached the rear of the newspaper where readers were promised an episode called "Requiem For A Head", an everyday tale of suburban schoolgoing tomfoolery. The teaser read, "When young Tommy Greene dies transporting explosives, one of Headmaster O'Mahony's best teachers comes under suspicion." When 9.20 arrived the station substituted "Love Is The Answer", the altogether more edifying story of life in an Italian boys' town founded by a Dublin priest.

The "deferral" came too late for one of the actors in the series who required medical treatment after, as the *Evening Press* elegantly put it, he was "thumped by a fat elderly lady". A few days after the axing the nation awoke to the headline "JB MURRAY IS BACK IN HOSPITAL". The unfortunate moralist was not much longer for this world. "The Spike" itself was bundled away like a demented auntie who has to be locked in the attic for the greater good. There it stays.

SHRUBS WERE ALSO PULLED UP

Peter Robinson Vs Inadequate Border Security 1986

"ULSTER HAS AWAKENED" was the slogan of the hour. In reality, though, the North's belligerent tribalism was just doing a spot of sleepwalking south of the border.

It was August 1986, the height of the Loyalist marching season. The Democratic Unionist Party's Peter Robinson had recently issued a dire warning that "the hour of politics is past" in the fight against the hated Anglo-Irish Agreement. The hour for bedtime was well past in the sleepy Monaghan village of Clontibret when a large invading force struck. The intruders were kitted out with "paramilitary-type jackets, masks and balaclavas and were carrying sticks and cudgels."

The mob marched, military style, three times around the village, daubing graffito and making a general nuisance of themselves. They blocked the Dublin road. They tore the Garda insignia from the wall of the village station. "Shrubs," noted the *Irish Times*, "were also pulled up." Two uniformed Gardai who attempted to intervene were set upon and beaten. Plain clothes reinforcements eventually sent the invaders scurrying back towards the border by firing pistols over their heads.

Habitually dapper Peter Robinson was wearing a navy jacket with the hood pulled up when Gardai plucked him from the retreating ranks. Things weren't how they looked, explained the Member of Parliament. The object of the exercise was to expose inadequate border security. The mob which penetrated into Clontibret unchallenged had actually provided a valuable public service. As for Robinson himself, he was only there in an observer capacity.

Overnighting at Monaghan Garda Station, the captive refused food and "Barry's tea", a calculated snub to Irish Foreign Minister and tea tycoon Peter Barry. Robinson broke his fast the following afternoon when his wife, Iris, brought him "good wholesome food from home." The stroll into Clontibret had produced some cases of swollen feat. Gardai and RUC numbered the marchers at a maximum of two hundred. Speaking from his cell, the MP reckoned there'd been five hundred. Meanwhile the DUP's Nigel Dodds triumphantly cited "one thousand men".

Robinson's incarceration threatened to prevent him making a speech in the Northern village of Keady that evening. A planned Orange procession through Keady had been banned by the RUC. Orangemen were going to assemble irrespective. Robinson wanted to be there. Iris complained that her husband's release was being deliberately delayed. She contended that the banning of the march in the first place was an RUC "surrender" to "sectarian bigotry".

Robinson was told to remove his "ULSTER SAYS NO" lapel badge before entering Ballybay District Court that evening. Once inside the courtroom the badge reappeared. He pleaded not guilty on all charges. Bail was set at £10,000. Robinson's team had anticipated only half that amount. The judge allotted half-an-hour to raise the shortfall. With five minutes to spare, the DUP's Rev. William McCrea arrived clutching a bag containing sterling, punts and travellers cheques. Liberated, Robinson hastened North to give his speech. His words failed to prevent a riot in Keady that night. In their efforts to resolve a tense situation, frustrated Loyalists left no stone unhurled.

Displaying instincts more suited to big fight promotion than the efficient dispensation of justice, the Republic's authorities chose Dundalk as the setting for Robinson's next court appearance. The defendant pondered wryly, "why it should be that my court case should be in a town that the world knows is an IRA dormitory town." Close friends advised him to stay home on the date of his court appearance but Deuteronomy and Genesis argued otherwise. Divine scripture told Peter Robinson "that I should go to that other land".

Decision made, associates urged him to at least wear a bullet-proof vest for the occasion. He preferred to place his trust in The Lord. "The guidance was clear," he later reflected, "and it would have showed a lack of faith if I was going to wear it." On the question of whether Jesus would have led marchers into Clontibret in the dead of night, he had no doubts. "Jesus Christ disliked evil as much as the Protestant community dislike evil," he stated. He didn't like the way that ecumenical churchmen "would try to make Jesus Christ into some kind of namby-pamby."

The DUP mobilised for a day-trip. Activist Jim Wells explained, "We will be there to stand between a baying horde of Sinn Fein people and Mr. Robinson... We will not be there to antagonise foreign subjects." Setting out in bullish mood, Mr. Wells told his troops, "If any foreign Paddies want to try to interfere with us we're ready for them." A hundred yards into the Republic the Unionist convoy pulled over so that Jim Wells could address the Paddy press.

"What's the feeling...", a reporter began.

"Fenians, did you say something about Fenians?" snapped Wells.

Jim Wells' suspicions were well founded. According to several news reports, the crowd gathered in Dundalk was indeed of the "baying" variety. The most anticipated scrap since Ali Vs. Forman duly got underway. After several rounds of bloody street scuffles, the lobbing of a crate of Republican petrol bombs and scenes of wanton vandalism in a car-park, the Loyalist visitors vamoosed without an intact no-claims bonus between them. And after all that, Robinson was simply remanded to Ballybay District Court for an October hearing.

Several adjournments later, the circus came to Dublin's Central Criminal Court in January 1987. On day three of the trial, the MP changed his plea to guilty on the first charge of unlawful assembly. Ten other charges of assault and causing malicious damage were dropped.

After a night in jail awaiting sentence, Robinson stood in the Green Street dock where the brave but inept proto-Republican Robert Emmet had famously demanded that no man write his epitaph until the Union be sundered. Mr. Justice Robert Barr raised eyebrows by suggesting that he felt the defendant was right. As in, Far Right. A "senior extremist politician" to be precise. He promptly withdrew the "extremist" bit after heated exchanges with Robinson's outraged counsel.

Justice Barr appeared to be enjoying the cut and thrust of the engagement. Robinson stated that he hadn't noticed anything odd about the Clontibret tour party - that they were wearing masks, for instance. The judge thought this strange, "particularly and ironically in that he was there as an observer". Robinson remained impassive throughout. Almost. According to one report, "The composure cracked for just a few seconds and he appeared visibly shaken" when the judge said that his role in the invasion merited "a substantial term of imprisonment." Robinson was acutely aware that a sentence of more than one year would automatically disqualify him from his Westminster seat and bar him from standing in the next British election.

He needn't have worried. The judge fined him £15,000, plus £2,588 damages. He was bound over to the peace for ten years. The *Irish Independent* reported that a few loiterers jeered as he left Green Street court with his "well-attired and striking" wife, "Irish". News of Robinson's punishment crossed the border. Word of his guilty plea apparently didn't. The Orange Order warned citizens of the Republic to stay out of the North following the "savage" penalty imposed on "a totally innocent man".

And a man of conviction to boot, as decided by an Irish court.

COUP D'ETAT OF THE YAHOOS

The Minister Of Defence Vs. The President 1976

If they only knew it, a lot of people had good reason to curse the name Cearbhall O'Dalaigh. As Chairman of the Commission on Income Taxation, he was chief architect of the iniquitous and hated PAYE open-prison system. However, by late 1976, after almost two years as President of Ireland, it was generally agreed that O'Dalaigh was doing a fine job. A font of culture and erudition, the President had been putting his multi-lingual skills to good use on a series of high-visibility friendship visits to Ireland's new EEC partners.

But admiration for the cosmopolitan head of state wasn't universal. O'Dalaigh had become President without an election in 1974. Fianna Fail had proposed him. Taoiseach Liam Cosgrave had accepted the nomination reluctantly. Cosgrave's Fine Gael were in government with Labour. It was an uneasy right-left balancing act. If Fine Gael had contested the Presidency, Labour would have been obliged to follow suit. The government was succeptible to a stress fracture. O'Dalaigh got the nod as a non-party candidate, but for some Fine Gaelers with long memories the new President came with a flawed pedigree. Back in the Forties he'd stood for election to the Dail as a Fianna Failer.

A former Chief Justice and twice Attorney General, President O'Dalaigh knew a thing or two about the law. He was particularly keen on human rights and civil liberties. Back in 1971 he'd made a daring suggestion that Ireland could benefit from importing various progressive European and UN conventions into the law of the land. O'Dalaigh became President at a time when the Cosgrave government was drafting reams of legislation clamping down on personal liberties under the slogan of "law and order".

In March of 1976 the President referred the government's Criminal Law (Jurisdiction) Act to the Supreme Court to test its constitutionality. It passed the test and he promptly signed it into law. Whatever his personal feelings, Justice Minister Cooney put a brave face on the intervention. Better to have the Act tried out by the President, he said, than by someone with a serious charge hanging over their head.

Then, in September 1976, O'Dalaigh did it again. This time he had reservations about the government's Emergency Powers Bill which allowed a person to be detained for up to seven days without being told why. Again, the bill was found to be constitutional and the President signed it into law at midnight on Saturday, 16th October 1976. His reservations about the legislation had delayed its passage by perhaps a month. He'd only been doing his job. For some members of the government, however, he was becoming a major pain in the Aras.

Precisely thirty-six hours after the bill was signed, the Minister For Defence, Paddy Donegan, arrived at Columb Army Barracks in Mullingar. The Minister was there to open a new cookhouse and mess hall. Members of the national press had travelled long distances for what was clearly not a major state occasion. They'd been tipped off that Minister Donegan would be taking a worthwhile detour from his script. The newshounds weren't short-changed.

"It was amazing when the President sent the Emergency Powers Bill to the Supreme Court," blustered the Minister. A brief rant followed. The Minister concluded with the declaration that, "In my opinion he is a thundering disgrace." At least, that's how the newspapers reported the phrase. Later that year O'Dalaigh would tell a dinner party that the exact words used were "a thundering bollocks". Minister Donegan was addressing an Army assembly. The object of his damnation, by dint of the Irish Constitution, was Commander-In-Chief of the Army. Paddy Donegan had dipped an elbow in political hot water before, but this was a breath-taking triple-somersault from the high-board.

The Oireachtas in 1976 was still a safe haven for a whole menagerie of "colourful" deputies, but some of Donegan's utterances had an eerie glow-in-the-dark quality that was all their own. He was fond of telling people that the Irish Navy was several hands short of a full deck, and, indeed, several decks short of an effective fleet. While this was undoubtedly true, it was thought unseemly for a Defence Minister to slag off his own forces. When the gun-running ship, Claudia, was intercepted, some felt the Minister's response failed to reflect the gravity of the situation. He recommended "a boot up the transom" for the arms smugglers. His cure for unemployment - put the jobless in the Army - was never enshrined in official government policy.

The Fianna Fail opposition wanted Donegan's head on a spike. Instead, they got an apology-cum-excuse from the Government Information Service on the Minister's behalf. It merely said, "I regret the remarks which arose out of my deep feelings for the security of our citizens. I intend to offer my apologies to the President as soon as possible."

The President, though, wouldn't play ball. The next morning, Tuesday, a government spokesman announced that Minister Donegan had left a Cabinet meeting to go to Aras An Uachtarain. An hour later there was still no sign of the Minister at the Presidential residence. The official story had to be changed. Forget the first announcement. The Minister was in his office and would visit the President later. Tea-time arrived and another statement was issued. The Minister was still in his office where he'd written a letter of apology which was now being delivered to the President by special messenger.

Apart from giving Donegan the cold shoulder, there was little the President could do by way of public rebuke. He was gagged by the Constitution. In certain circumstances, on a matter of national or public importance, the President could address the nation. Or both Houses of the Oireachtas, which was pretty much the same thing. Trouble was, whatever he said would have to be vetted and approved in advance by the same government from whence the affront came.

While President O'Dalaigh played hard to get, Fianna Fail tabled a Dail motion calling on the Taoiseach to seek his Defence Minister's resignation. Fianna Fail leader Jack Lynch added that he did so with regret, and that no way was he seeking party political gain from the issue. Taoiseach Cosgrave replied that he was happy with Donegan's written apology to the President. Fianna Fail's Des O'Malley was decidedly unhappy with it. He described Donegan's attack as "unfortunate and idiotic".

Fine Gael's John Kelly mounted an imaginative interpretation of what had happened. Kelly argued that the President's position in public life made him vulnerable to criticism. The weight of mathematical probability dictated that some of that criticism was bound to be unwarranted dog rot. The Minister's remarks were the result of strong, although completely wrong, feelings. The outburst was simply evidence of his "passionate commitment" to his job. Donegan's astounding swipe at the Head Of State was best regarded as "the product of a hot and generous temperament".

A vote was taken. The Dail motion for Donegan's resignation was defeated by a margin of five. Seven Fianna Fail deputies didn't vote because of a pre-arranged "pairing" with seven absent government members, including Donegan. The *Irish Times* was dismayed at the outcome. In its best headmasterly tone the paper scolded, "It was shameful that the Taoiseach could bring himself to do no more than mumble a half-hearted apology to the President. It was shameful that the Minister for Defence, having failed to resign, should not at least have come into the House and made a manly apology to his peers... A bad day's work was done for democracy yesterday."

The government had made its choice. Donegan stayed. The President called their bluff. The day after the Dail vote, O'Dalaigh resigned. The Cabinet was given a bare ten minutes notice before the President went public with his decision. A civilian once more, O'Dalaigh could now embarrass Donegan by releasing the texts of the Minister's apology, together with the dismissive snub it earned. "Have you any conception," he'd chided, "of your responsibilities?" The government responded to the shock resignation with a hollow statement deeply regretting the President's decision and adding how much it appreciated his services to the country.

On December 3rd 1976, Patrick Hillary succeeded Cearbhall O'Dalaigh as Head Of State. As was usual, the electorate had no say in the matter. The day before the new President took office, Liam Cosgrave reshuffled his cabinet. Paddy Donegan was relieved of his Defence duties and packed off to the more tranquil pastures of the Lands Department. To many, it looked as if the so-called "coup d'état of the Yahoos" had claimed its final victim.

I WILL HAVE YOU SHOT

Alex Higgins Vs. Dennis Taylor 1990

It was billed as the OK Corral of the green baize. The fixture itself was of modest import, a quarter-final tie in the 1990 Irish Masters at Goffs. But this time Alex Higgins had really, seriously, gone beyond the beyond. Mild-mannered Dennis Taylor was gunning for him.

Only six days earlier the pair had been team-mates in the Northern Ireland side which had contested the final of snooker's World Cup. Higgins, Taylor and third man Tony Murphy presented a picture of beaming harmony during their run of victories in the competition. Then, within minutes of their defeat by Canada in the decider, the chummy facade disintegrated in a sudden eruption of searing bile.

The tremors had begun the previous evening. Having just won their Semi-Final, the Northern Ireland trio posed for photographs. Higgins picked that moment to tell Murphy, "You played like a shit". Team spirit wasn't improved the following afternoon when, during the first session of the Final match, Higgins hijacked two frames allotted to Taylor. Taylor and Murphy bit their tongues and twiddled their thumbs, "just to keep peace and quiet".

That fragile peace and quiet was in smithereens mere moments after Canada's victory. Higgins tore into Taylor with a torrent of verbal abuse. Taylor understandably declined to share a press conference platform with his antagonist. An emotional Higgins went on a solo run before the media audience, accusing his team-mate of wanton greed. Taylor had stood to collect a £6,000 bonus for the highest break of the tournament. That prize had been snatched away in the very last frame of the night when one of the Canadians nullified Taylor's modest 71 with an unbroken 124.

Higgins was furious that Taylor had intended keeping the hypothetical bonus prize. "I've known this guy for twenty-four years," he squawked. "I didn't know anybody could be that greedy. He has put money before everything, he has put money before his country. In my estimation, Taylor is not a snooker player, because the more money he gets the more he wants."

The Hurricane raged hard. "I'm absolutely disgusted with him," stormed Higgins, "and he doesn't deserve to wear the badge which shows the Red Hand of Ulster. If he ever speaks to me again I will pretend to be deaf and dumb. I gave him my room number at the hotel if he wanted to get into fisticuffs. We've had a fabulous week in Bournemouth, but there has just been one fly in the ointment and he comes from the pits of Coalisland." With that, Higgins announced that he was off to a nightclub.

Taylor then returned to have his say. He told astounded journalists that Higgins had threatened him. His exact words had been, "I come from Shankhill, you come from Coalisland and the next time you are in Northern Ireland I will have you shot." Taylor was horrified, less by the shadow of the gunman than by Higgins' invocation of sectarian hatred. Scrupulously apolitical, Taylor prided himself on his hard-won cross-community esteem.

Taylor revealed that, "During the first session interval of the final, Alex even dragged Tony and myself into the Ladies' toilet for a team talk. A lady came in and Alex told her to go to the gents. Alex called me a thirteen-and-a-half stone bag of shit and said that he wanted me back in his hotel room to sort out the problems." Crude remarks about Taylor's late mother had really twisted the knife.

And as for the £6,000 that never was. Taylor said that the Northern Ireland team had a long-standing agreement that in such cases the winner takes all. "It was Alex's idea in the first place," he stated, adding, "I'm supposed to be the captain of the team, but we have always gone along with Alex rather than cause the team to be in disarray."

Taylor was at a complete loss. He'd helped out Higgins in the past. He'd tried to see the best in his capricious team-mate. "You grin and bear it for all those years," he sighed, "then you get this thrown at you". Throwing was by now second nature to Higgins. A year previously, police had been called to the star's Manchester flat complex during a protracted bout of furniture flinging in a blazing row with his girlfriend. The police were questioning neighbours when they saw Higgins plunging Earthwards past their window. Incredibly, he survived the mysterious fall from his second-floor window with negligible injuries. "He was paralytic," observed a neighbour. Days before his World Cup outburst he'd been fined £50 for hurling a skateboard through an ex-wife's window when she refused to let him deliver presents to his kids.

"I'll never speak to him again," insisted Taylor, irritated that "The majority of people side with him because they don't know what sort of person he is. If they did, he wouldn't get the support he does." Higgins' support was indeed phenomenal. His speed, skill and audacity had once transported the game to a new dimension. Twice a world champion, he was the sport's first and greatest people's hero. Insiders knew better. Higgins was widely despised by his peers. In the words of Stephen Hendry's manager, Ian Doyle: "With Higgins around the tension quadruples. He poisons the atmosphere."

Now, even the public could see it. The crowd at Goffs froze him out for the first time ever. They cheered Taylor, who studiously ignored his opponent throughout a dull contest. As if sensing he was on a hiding to nothing, Higgins meekly capitulated.

The Higgins-Taylor bust-up was another painful round in the sorry saga of Higgins Vs. Higgins. In 1972 The Hurricane captured the World Championship with a flair never witnessed before or since. A decade later, in 1982, he again lifted the crown in dashing style. Fifteen years on, he sank seven pints and little else while crashing out of a qualifying match five games removed from a first round appearance in the 1997 competition.

A long time on the ropes, The Hurricane was sliding groggily towards the canvas. He'd been rooming in a cheap hotel, his rent paid from a benevolent fund set up to aid players who'd fallen upon "genuine hardship". On the eve of his latest humiliation he'd been turfed out of his lodgings for disruptive behaviour. Somewhere, somehow, he'd squandered some two million pounds along the way.

While he searched for a new digs, the BBC began filming a new series entitled "Senior Pot Black", showcasing a dozen of snooker's first television stars. Alex Higgins had been the brightest of them all. For him, the call never came.

THE SCHEDULE ENDED WITH 'CLOSEDOWN'

Century Radio Vs. The Slippery Slope 1989-91

Century Radio was talked up as a chrome-finished megastore on Ireland's infotainment superhighway, retailing alluring new lines in consumer choice. The mundane reality didn't take long to sink in. Century was a political football with a slow puncture. Aptly, the station's sorry saga became inextricably linked with the Quixotic quest for "a level playing field".

Century's brief was to compete with RTE Radio One and the recently refurbished 2FM for a national audience. This was assumed to be something of a cinch. But as the game wore on with Century increasingly pinned back in their own box, the tilt of the playing surface took on an obsessional significance for them and their committed band of supporters.

As Minister for Communications, Ray Burke commandeered the twin roles of referee and groundsman. He tried to steamroller the playing surface flat. He awarded hotly disputed decisions in Century's favour. He disallowed seemingly perfectly good efforts by RTE. When all else failed, he launched a ferocious Cantonaesque drop-kick that left the Montrose outfit bruised and confused. But the Minister's radio interference only postponed the inevitable...

It had all started so promisingly. The pirates had been banished from the airwaves by law on December 31st, 1988, leaving the way open for a new breed of radio entrepreneur to print their own money. Or so it seemed. The Dublin superpirates had opened lucrative veins of advertising revenue, making radio look like the sexiest get-rich-quick scheme in town. It seemed that a nationwide legitimate version would slip into a First Class carriage on the gravy train.

Concert promoter Oliver Barry and hotelier Jim Stafford raised the bulk of the early investment, bringing on board high-profile directors Terry Wogan, with a 5% interest, and Chris De Burgh with half that. The consortium attempted to poach several of RTE's top celebrities with offers of big money and creative input, but their only sizeable catch was Marty Whelan. The new station's news department fared better, wresting away the formidable RTE trio of Caroline Erskine, Jackie Hayden and David Davin Power. Richard Crowley also transferred from the RTE newsroom to take on an entertainment brief at Century.

Smart new premises were secured overlooking Dublin's Christchurch Cathedral and grandly christened The Century Pavilion. Century went on the air at 8am, September 4th, 1989. The first words heard on the new service were, "Good morning. Cead failte go leir. This is Terry Wogan." Prophetically, it was a taped message. The first disc spun was U2's "Pride".

Terry Wogan was present in the flesh for a swish launch brunch. Wogan cracked jokes and emphasised that Century would be operating "without a safety net". RTE, by implication, had heaps of licence-fee safety-netting stashed up their end of the uneven pitch. Still, Terry stressed that RTE and Century must co-operate, on the grounds that "this country is too small to have two broadcasting organisations trying to kill each other." Some hope. Minister Burke had already antagonised RTE by siding with Century in a row over how much the new station should pay RTE for transmitting its signal. Burke ordered RTE to settle for what it deemed an unrealistically low offer from Century.

The launch was a pleasantly delusional affair. Ray Burke was like a kid with a new toy. "It's a great day lads," he chirruped, "a great day. It's a great day, great to be alive and great to be in government." Chris De Burgh, too, seemed to have greatness on his mind - his own. The diminutive doggerel dispenser let it be known that while he was more accustomed to creating the "oxygen" that radio listeners breathe, he was proud to be associated with this "vigorous" new venture.

But when the champagne glasses were cleared away and the bunting came down, the cracks in Century's spanking new broadcasting edifice became quickly and ominously apparent. The station's catchphrase was "radio like you've never heard it before". For many parts of the country, though, Century was "radio like you've never heard it at all". The station promised its advertisers Day One coverage across 60% of the population. It achieved 35%. Transmission equipment squabbles and shortfalls led to an arrested development from which Century never recovered.

Those who could tune in encountered little to glue their ears. RTE's radio boss, Kevin Healy, had dismissed the newcomer with the curt criticism that Century was "strong on cash but short on new ideas and new talent." Events proved Healy right. Unable to lure the really big names from RTE, the station was severely charasmatically challenged. Radio programmers, not broadcasters, had dominated the pirates. The legacy of the clutter-free buccaneers was a paucity of accomplished talking heads. Century had to fish in a very shallow pool of talent.

Granted, Century's news and current affairs coverage was top-notch, but so too was RTE's, and RTE had tried and trusted names like Gaybo, Pat Kenny, Marian Finucane and Gerry Ryan. When Terry Wogan got the weather laughably wrong, the station's star vehicle was found out as a dodgy second-hand import. People felt conned, goodwill evaporated. Marty Whelan stepped into the breach left by Wogan, ringing up brides on their way to the altar as sure proof of the show's nowness. But the damage was done. Soon, Emer Woodfull's mid-morning magazine slot shrivelled up and died in the airless shadow of Gaybo and Gerry Ryan. Century waved the white flag in that battle and concentrated their efforts elsewhere. There was still a whole war to lose.

As the months ticked by, the scale of Century's miscalculations seemed more and more monumental. What should have been a nice little earner was fast turning into a financial abyss. The signal wasn't all there. Century's ill-mapped middle road between Radio One and 2FM had attracted few fellow travellers. It had taken 2FM ten years of trial and (mostly) error to get the balance right as a national presence. Century had expected to slip comfortably into the shoes of the pirates, but there had never been a national pirate. The advertisers became restless, then mutinous. With sharpened hindsight, there were mutterings that the station had pitched itself awry from the outset - that its besuited, corporate image was a major turn-off with Middle Ireland.

During its first eight months on the air, Century lost an estimated £3,000,000. The IRTC had granted Barry, Stafford *et al* their licence under the normal business understanding that

Century's management would do their sums and reap the benefits. The playing field had seemed level enough after Minister Burke gave Century the nod in the transmission fees dispute, but by the summer of 1990 every bump and divot was being pored over by anxious souls wielding spirit-levels.

There were several compelling reasons why Minister Burke should use all his might to rescue Century, quite apart from the entente cordial which prevailed between Fianna Fail and the Barry-Stafford axis. Century was the golden child of Burke's 1988 Broadcasting Act, its frailty left him open to accusations of negligent parenting. Additionally, there was bad blood between Fianna Fail and RTE. Fianna Fail blamed RTE's coverage of the 1989 general election, and particularly that of Radio One, for the party's poor showing which had imposed the indignity of coalition. Whether RTE's hostility was real or imagined, Fianna Fail desperately wanted an alternative national broadcast news service.

Burke's hamfisted excavations on the playing pitch made a martyr of RTE and lost Century the few friends it had left. Having stated in 1988 that "it would be entirely inappropriate to spend public money" on the new profit-driven independents, the Minister now proposed to give Century part of RTE's license fee. The political and financial machinations of the Burke/ Century/2FM love-hate triangle are tortuous, but Dublin was the key. Century had less than 10% of the 15-34 Dublin audience which was crucial to solvency.

Through the Independent Radio and Television Commission (IRTC), the two Dublin independent stations - 98FM and Capital - had legally enforceable contracts. RTE's music station, 2FM, only had the protection of public opinion. Minister Burke effectively tried to kill off 2FM to save Century. On the eve of 2FM's eleventh birthday, Ray Burke unveiled plans to transform the station into an "education and public information" service. His vision for the pop station included providing instruction in "continental languages, the Irish language, the rural and farming sectors, business and trade union affairs, social welfare and social affairs."

Flabbergasted, 2FM boss Cathal McCabe had to laugh. He registered his contempt by issuing an internal circular requiring

DJs to translate a passage of Hungarian, draught a request for headage payments, and pencil-in three suggested halting sites on a map of Dalkey. That sort of thing. Fine Gael's Jim Mitchell charged that Minister Burke was "screwing" 2FM by trying to turn it into "a drudge station". The stars of RTE descended on Leinster House to protest their dismay. Gay Byrne and Gerry Ryan's shows were swamped with angry calls.

As the debate raged, Ray Burke shot himself in the foot. He turned up at Century to present his own show, a xerox of "Desert Island Discs". Just before he went on air the 2FM news was piped into the station. Gerry Ryan was heard inciting the nation to "give it to him between the eyes". Burke's pompous Century broadcast only served to harden public opinion against him. One critic observed that the Minister was "trying to give the impression that he was somehow a great rock'n'roller and ex-hippy... The show came across as arrogant and enormously patronising."

Some of the mud slung at Burke stuck to Century. The old 2FM catchphrase "Cominatcha" was amended to "Cumainn-atcha" in deference to the station's perceived cavortings with Fianna Fail. One publication printed up a suggested new schedule for Century. It included: 6am "Burke's Law" with Ray Burke; 8am "What It Says In The Papers" with government press secretary PJ Mara; 10pm "Thought For The Day" with Charles Haughey. Today's thought: "I wouldn't half mind pushing that fucker over a cliff." Pointedly, the schedule ended with "Closedown"...

The public uproar was sufficient to send Burke scurrying down an alternative path. He capped RTE's advertising revenue in order to free up moolah for other media. Century had a reprieve. Trouble was, by now, many advertisers wouldn't touch the ailing station with a thousand foot mast.

Things were going from bad to worse. At the very time Ray Burke was courting public odium in his bid to salvage Century's news service, that service went off the air. The inevitable advertising response to the station's paucity of listeners had led to severe belt-tightening. The first staff lay-offs came just three months into Century's short life. In June 1990, with Century's woes making the news, its own newsroom went on strike over cutbacks and under-resourcing. Meanwhile RTE began milking public sympathy for their own government sponsored plight. It was even put about that Dinny's famous fry-ups on the set of the "Glenroe" TV soap would be nixed as an energy-saving measure.

Century was slowly gaining market share, but after a year on the air it desperately needed a fresh injection of capital. It got an injection of Capital. London's Capital Radio bought into the ailing station and provided a £1.8m fillip that persuaded other investors to top up the total to £3.2m. But Capital wouldn't settle for a silent partnership, and the backs-to-the-wall camaraderie which had sustained Century's staff morale soured into an Us-Against-Them situation.

Catherine Maher had been with Century from the start. She recalled, "When Capital installed their people, that was the cataclysmic point of no return. These Brit programme controllers came over and fucked around with the programming." Dolores Keane was out, Pet Shop Boys and blip-hop were in. Many of Century's seasoned hands were bypassed. Maher recalled, "The whole English/Irish question raised itself in a subtle way. It was unspoken, but there was an underlying feeling of cultural imperialism, and there was a resentment there."

The deckchairs on the Titanic were duly rearranged and Century became Century FM. While the country's milking parlours and building sites came to terms with a diet of gay disco, Century's troubleshooters evidently decided that there was no percentage in fighting a losing battle against RTE's better-resourced news and current affairs service. In April 1991 the new management moved to rip out the backbone of their news department. David Davin Power, Caroline Erskine and Jackie Hayden were given their marching orders. The trio resisted, but in vain. Incredibly, Century told the Independent Radio & Television Commission that the sackings wouldn't effect the station's solemn commitment to meeting its statuary 20% news quota. The IRTC, it seemed, could like it or lump it.

Century FM stumbled aimlessly past its second birthday, demoralised, downsized and dismal. By late 1991 the station claimed about 18% of the national radio audience, half its original projection. Century was in a chronic negative equity situation - for every £3 the station spent it was earning £2. On November 6th Oliver Barry announced that he'd availed of "an attractive offer" for his stake in the company and was bailing out. Century's remaining top brass responded with the dreaded vote of confidence. Assurances were given that "arrangements have been made for the injection of £1.542 million into the company."

A fortnight later, Century FM went out with a whimper. At 6pm on November 19th, 1991, the plug was pulled on the comatose patient. It transpired that Capital had wanted to increase their shareholding from their existing 30% to 50%, despite the fact that, as a foreign investor, they already owned in excess of the legally-permitted 28%. Having tolerated a bending of the rules the last time, the IRTC put its foot down. Capital pulled out, Century shut down.

Century's programme controller, Paul Cooney, marked the station's passing with the rueful epitaph that "the level playing field never materialised". The station's fifty numbed staffers dispersed quietly, some never to be heard of again. A few prodigal sons and daughters eventually straggled back towards Montrose where they were put on latrine detail until something better came up.

Century had the unique distinction of being greatly missed during its lifetime, but not at all in death. In sickness and ill-health it failed in its avowed purpose to pioneer a fresh course for Irish radio. Indeed, for its unremitting pursuit of the mythic Level Playing Field, Century will be vaguely remembered as a Flat Earth movement hopelessly doomed to extinction in a world of slippery slopes.

THERE ARE CERTAIN THINGS IN LIFE THAT CERTAIN OTHER THINGS DON'T APPLY TO

Ken McCue Vs The Community Of Faith 1992-93

Dubliner Ken McCue started his secondary education left-handed and finished it ambidextrous. Far from being grateful to the Christian Brothers for putting him right, McCue took away a lifetime resentment of their school-of-hard-knocks regime.

By the time he'd reached his mid-thirties, Ken McCue had been a devout atheist for more years than he cared to remember. In the late Eighties, he wrote to the Archbishop Of Dublin seeking to cancel his membership of the Catholic Church. He waited for a reply. And waited. And waited. McCue let the matter slide until a brief encounter with the hospital system pushed it back onto the agenda. Someone, he discovered, had taken the liberty of listing his religion as "RC" on his admission card. After an earnest appeal, the entry was erased.

Two weeks later, Ken was back at the hospital for tests. He noticed that he was listed on the computer register as Roman Catholic. He asked the registrar to change the entry. The nearest category to "Atheist" on the hospital system was "Agnostic", charitably suggesting that the barer of the label is confused rather than damned.

Stung into action by his hospital experience, McCue again attempted to formalise his defection from the church which had claimed him as an infant. It was late 1992. He tendered a letter of resignation to the offices of the Catholic Archbishop of Dublin. The Archbishop's newly installed Chancellor sent a prompt acknowledgement, enclosing a 22-page internal discussion paper to illuminate McCue's position.

From the document, McCue discovered that the Church of Rome, in common with another celebrated Italian fraternity, doesn't let its initiates walk away lightly. The paper was firm on this point: "Loss of faith, for example, does not result in a loss of membership. The Catholic Church still claims jurisdiction over all those baptised in the Catholic Church or received into it (Canon II)... It by no means follows that because the subject is instrumental in forging membership that he also has the capacity to dissolve it." Ken McCue believed his membership had indeed been forged, while he was an innocent lullaby-stander at the baptismal font. He eventually found a get-out clause.

Ken learned that he could make a "formal act of defection" by uttering heretical pronouncements or by "notorious rejection". The latter option entails making a public and hostile repudiation of Catholicism. Even at this break point in the relationship, the Church reserves the right to refuse a divorce. In the words of the document, "Church involvement and analysis of the act must inevitably become part of the process... The will of the agent alone effects nothing at the visible juridical level."

In summation, the paper suggested that the best thing for disaffected Catholics to do was to tender "an application informing or requesting church authorities of departure." The Church could then launch "an investigation to determine what weight should be given to the application." This investigation "would normally involve requesting an interview with the applicant... in the course of which one could discover whether or not the request is genuine, or that of a disturbed or perhaps annoyed person." This implicit admission that the Church cherished "disturbed" members over ones who knew their minds confirmed McCue's decision to quit.

An interview was duly arranged for the beginning of 1993. The Chancellor of the House of the Archbishop of Dublin welcomed Ken into the Archbishop's Palace. The Chancellor explained that common-or-garden unchristian behaviour doesn't disqualify anyone from Church membership. "The Church is essentially a community of faith," he said, "and it doesn't at all follow that you're going to necessarily measure up in your actual behaviour." We are all sinners, but the Church extends "an invitation to live in a particular kind of way."

The Chancellor outlined four possible avenues of defection open to McCue. He could embrace a different religion. He could voluntarily sign a renunciation of the Catholic faith. He could post a formal affidavit of defection. Or he could make a solemn profession of atheism before witnesses.

McCue told the Chancellor that he very much liked the sound of the solemn profession before witnesses. By its very nature, atheism lacked the opportunities for social get-togethers that the members of organised religions took for granted. Ken told the Chancellor he wanted to go public. The Archbishop's man expressed stern disapproval. No-one in Ireland had ever done such a thing.

The Chancellor attempted to establish why, precisely, his visitor was so anxious to quit the Church. McCue replied that there were various articles of faith he just couldn't get his head around, like the existence of angels, the infallibility of the Pope and the sacrament of transubstantiation where bread and wine become the body and blood of Christ. The Chancellor granted that there would be scientific problems with the latter but that "there are certain things in life that certain other things just don't apply to". So there.

Shot down over transubstantiation, McCue bounced back with a demarcation dispute. Why, he asked, does the Lord's Prayer involve the faithful asking God to "lead us not into temptation". Surely, said Ken, leading us into temptation was strictly the Devil's business? The Chancellor replied that Jesus told us to pray in that manner, end of story.

The Chancellor drew the discussion to a close by urging Ken to "think it over" for a while before doing anything drastic. McCue brought the tape he'd covertly made of the conversation to a journalist who wrote up the story. Meanwhile, Ken sent a letter to the Chancellor seeking to set a date for his formal profession of atheism before witnesses. He got no reply. McCue phoned the Chancellor, who registered intense displeasure at the publication of the article. He was not willing to discuss setting a date.

Since then, McCue has sent several more letters to the Archbishop's Palace without reply. His continued detention in the Lord's mansion of many rooms put him in mind of a couple of hotels. One was Fawlty Towers. The other was The Eagles' "Hotel California", a place where - as the song famously puts it - "You can check out any time you like, but you can never leave."

MORAL DEPRAVITY, MY LORD

Holy Ireland Vs. The Lesbian Nuns 1985

Friday the 13th of September 1985 was going to prove unlucky for one side in the tug-of-war for Ireland's immortal soul. The lesbian nuns were coming. After days of breathless speculation, a Thursday morning radio interview confirmed that lapsed Catholic sisters Nancy Manahan and Rosemary Curb would arrive the following day to plug their US best seller, "Breaking Silence - Lesbian Nuns On Convent Sexuality". An appearance on "The Late Late Show" was in prospect, although the programme had a policy of keeping its guest-list a secret until transmission time. Aghast protesters jammed the Montrose switch. Just in case.

What gave? The infamous Bishop And The Nightie scandal of two decades before had long acquired comedy cult status. Gaybo himself had interviewed a lesbian on the show six years back, eliciting barely a whimper of "Sodom and begorrah". But these were changed times. Here, at the mid-point of the Eighties, the rancour of the first abortion referendum still lingered, while the first divorce poll was bearing down hard. A state of most uncivil war obtained between Irelands old and new. And besides, lesbians were one thing, but lesbian nuns... Was nothing sacred?

On the Thursday morning of the radio interview, Dublin customs seized 1,500 copies of the offending book, seemingly unaware that 3,000 volumes were already on full frontal display in bookshops around the country. An official announcement was hurried out on Thursday night. Its tone was unmistakably one of "Oops, there's been a ghastly mistake". The seizure was pinned on a lone zealot. No need to panic. The impounded tomes had now been "cleared by reference to a higher authority".

The book itself chronicled the experiences of forty-nine nuns and former nuns across North America. Each had a remarkably similar story to tell. Namely, that "our devotion to our girlfriends and the nuns, along with our discomfort on dates with boys, was not, as we suspected at the time, an unmistakable sign of religious vocation, but a premonition of our late-blooming lesbianism." Dire warnings had been issued to novices about the dangers of forming 'particular friendships' with co-habitees, although no particulars were ever given.

A press conference was arranged for Buswell's hotel for three o'clock on the Friday afternoon. However, upon arrival there, the former sisters were flatly informed that the room they'd booked was unavailable. The authors, their publishers, a coterie of journalists and half of Dublin's gay community were summarily dispatched onto the street. There they remained for some time, hanging around. There was nowhere to go because it was the Holy Hour. A vengeful God couldn't have fashioned a more poetic justice. The Pink Elephant bar eventually provided a makeshift press HQ when the pubs readmitted at 3.30.

At this juncture the action shifted across town to the High Court where Thomas O'Mahony, a solicitor and director of the little-known Christian Community Centre, was seeking an injunction to keep the ex-nuns off the airwaves. O'Mahony argued that if the "Late Late" appearance went ahead, "it would greatly undermine Christian moral values in Irish society". In addition, he claimed, "the respect of the general public for nuns would be greatly undermined."

Justice Barr wasn't having any of it. He couldn't even ascertain for certain that RTE were going to interview the renegade sisters that night. In a nutshell, the judge decided that the arguments for the proposed ban amounted to too little too late. Justice Barr added: "RTE have in the past interviewed leading homosexuals, giving them the opportunity to express their views and explain their ..."

"Moral depravity, my lord" pressed O'Mahony.

In the hours before the show, RTE's top brass convened and gave the nuns their blessing. In a terse statement they said they were "satisfied that it will be presented in a responsible manner". Thomas O'Mahony was far from satisfied. Hotfoot from his failed High Court challenge he arrived outside RTE. There, in the words of the *Irish Press*, he "led the crowd outside the studio in reciting decades of the Rosary and in hymn singing".

The pocket-sized multitude in question consisted of the singing solicitor, Fianna Fail TD Michael Barrett, eighty civilians, several bull-horns and one portable Virgin Mary. Leaflets issued by Christian Community Action said the purpose of the high-decibel vigil was to persuade RTE "to desist from offending the Christian moral values of the Irish people by glamorising the heinous sin of Sodom and Gomorra". Mrs Elizabeth O'Hanlon, a "concerned mother of three" was worried that the item might put young girls off vocations. A number of callers to the station expressed the view that if Gay Byrne wanted to preside over this sort of heresy, he might consider a new career in the States.

The ex-nuns were visibly shaken by the hostility of the picket. In the face of adversity, Nancy Manahan gallantly turned the other cheek. She remarked, "I admire them for coming out to stand up for what they believe in. They too are breaking silence." Gaybo was more concerned with Christian activists breaking the law. Leaving the studio under Garda escort after the show he fulminated that, "During the past week there have been several threats on my life, on my children, on my wife and on my home."

The item itself was televised Purgatory, lacking any redeeming raciness. There were no lewd tales of cloistered capering, just a restrained five-way discussion radiating stifling sweetness and light. The phone calls to the station after the show were over-whelmingly sympathetic to the ex-nuns. Gaybo surmised that most viewers would have found the whole affair "very boring".

The day's escapades provided an excuse for a slew of "GAY AND LESBIANS" headlines in that weekend's newspapers. By Monday, normal service had been resumed. "NO MOVING STATUES, SAYS BISHOP" trumpeted the *Irish Press*. It was the start of another average week in inter-referenda Ireland.

A FINE VINDIFICATION

"Magill" Vs. Irish Irelandism 1977-90

Towards the end of the Seventies, the underground culture which had been gurgling faintly for a decade began to seep up between the flagstones of Irish life. Three new niche magazines sprang into existence within a year, each dedicated to putting counter-culture on the counter.

In Dublin appeared in 1976. It was pocket-sized, puny and studenty. *Hot Press* followed in mid-1977. Its in-depth coverage of The Boulder Band and Kate & Anna McGarragle was unrivalled. *Magill* arrived amid much fanfare in October 1977.

It was the time of punk. If *In Dublin* and *Hot Press* represented the upstart spirit of The Clash and The Sex Pistols (sizeable "if"), then *Magill* was Bob Dylan and Grecian 2000. The magazine's thrusting force was Vincent Browne, who'd distinguished himself as a cub reporter in Prague '68, with blow-by-blow accounts of how one strand of the putative World Revolution was coming unstuck. Joining Browne on *Magill*'s board of directors were Mary Holland, Noel Pearson and Bruce Arnold, all veterans of the struggle against entrenched Irish Irelandism.

Magill was an evolutionary freak, a brash hybrid of *Socialist Worker* and *Country Life*. Its unlikely make-up was an Irish solution to an Irish problem. The problem being that the centre in Irish politics stretched 360% until it overlapped itself (Labour had just emerged from four years in bed with Liam Cosgrave's ultra-reactionary FG). The new magazine was clearly of The Left, but it was anything but proletarian. A genuine socialist option in Ireland was firmly in view, just over there, nestling between full employment and the Olympic-sized swimming pool. In the meantime there was advertising space to be sold.

The advertisers had no doubts about which end of the socialist spectrum they were pitching at. There were no second-hand pigeon lofts or home-brew sets between the covers of the new magazine. *Magill*'s readers were targeted with financial advice, Waterford Crystal, Volvo cars, fine wines, luxury four-bedroomed houses, plays at The Abbey and oil paintings. Only the pink salmon was missing. There were other tell-tale signs that *Magill* was shaping up as the in-house organ of the West Brit condom-wearing set. An advert for "Family Planning Services" brazenly invited readers to "Call yourself or write for non-medical supplies".

Some hallowed *Magill* traditions were in place right from the start - the political keyhole surgery, the gratuitous sports feature and the standard urban blight time-bomb script (Inner city crime "just might not be containable any more" - G. Kerrigan). And then there was the "GOING OUT" section which occupied almost two-thirds of the magazine.

The *Magill* reader on the tiles in 1977 could consult Conor Cruise O'Brien on Theatre, Ulick O'Connor on Restaurants, Bruce Arnold on Art and Anthony Cronin on Pubs, with sundry mere mortals taking up the slack on Cinema, Environment and Music (Demis Roussos, Bernie Flint and Horslips were the hot tickets).

The most intriguing section of *Magill's* "GOING OUT" guide was the one entitled "PROTEST". Covering two full pages, the "PROTEST" listings were subdivided into four categories: "The Left", "Pressure Groups", "Women's Groups" and "Homosexual's Groups". Each dissident cell got a pithy write-up. The Irish Gay Rights Movement, for instance, "Seeks to break down anti-homosexual prejudice. Offers counsel to homosexuals and runs a disco".

The most extensive compartment of the "PROTEST" section was devoted to "The Left". This was clearly a labour of love. Every one-horse splinter group in town got a mention. The Liaison For The Left, The Connolly Youth Movement, The Movement For A Socialist Republic... nobody was left out. The entry for The League For A Workers' Republic was not untypical (deep breath): *"Trotskyist. All Trotskyist groups look to the Fourth International founded by Leon Trotsky in 1938 in opposition to the Second (Social Democratic) International and the Third (Communist) International. FI split in 1952 and again in 1963. Most Trotskyist groups adhere to one or other of the international tendencies sprouting from these splits. LWR is affiliated to the Organising Committee for the Reconstruction of the FI which believes that the fragmentation of Trotskyism is such that it is necessary to build again from the base. Calls for an all-Ireland*

'Constituent Assembly' and all-Ireland Labour Party. Publication Workers' Republic, bi-monthly. No address available."

Dang! So, only owners of crystal balls need apply. Perhaps joining a "Pressure Group" might be simpler. How about the Prisoners' Rights Organization, which "Holds that all crime is essentially political". Sounds good, until you read the next entry, advertising the Prisoners' Committee: "Breakaway from Prisoners' Rights Organization led by Brendan Walsh. Alleges Prisoners' Rights Organization is a front for Officials" (Sinn Fein The Workers Party, linked to Official IRA). Uh-uh…

Moving swiftly on, let's skip the "Women's Groups" section and look at the pictures. Nice colourful one there of some bare breasts from the movie "Valentino". Don't get many of them to the pound in Seventies' Ireland! Love the ad for the new Opel Manta: "Take her, and see how she is so beautifully endowed!" *Fworarr* missus!

Needless to say, this endearing hotch-potch of contradictions couldn't endure. By the mid-Eighties *Magill* had taken on the classic contours of its Golden Age. The GUBU years had been manna from Heaven for *Magill*. The national newspapers dutifully covered the stories of political skulduggery, but weren't half so quick to break them. Traditional party allegiances and a culture of lethargic complicity in the media left plenty of scope for a crusading organ with an appetite for spadework.

The tweedy veterans of the PROTEST era had given way to a squad of young tyros spearheaded by the likes of Fintan O'Toole, John Waters, Derek Dunne, Olivia O'Leary and Mark Brannock. With "accountability" and "transparency" the currency of the hour, the old-fashioned socialist cant was swept quietly under the carpet. Tellingly, when Noelle Campbell Sharp took *Magill* to court in 1985 over an alleged libel by Eamonn McCann, Vincent Browne attempted to mitigate McCann's case by pleading that "the author's preoccupation to liberate the working class leads him to be heavy handed."

The post-GUBU legacy was a deep and widespread distrust of politicians, which had more or less been *Magill*'s editorial line from day one. By a happy twist of circumstance, the magazine was voicing opinions that were both popular and profitable. In the mid-Eighties *Magill* scaled new twin peaks of moral high ground and prestige advertising revenue.

By now, the magazine had expanded far beyond its original "Dublin 4" constituency to become a truly national institution, with big doses of GAA coverage to prove it. There were other accommodations, like "Company Profile" puff pieces which smoothed the way for lucrative adverts for telex machines, office computers, credit cards, financial planning and duty free shopping.

But nobody bought *Magill* for its adverts, no matter how alluringly glossy. They bought it for interviews with people that - in the best interests of the public, of course - the national media wouldn't touch with a rolled up copy of Section 31. Like the eleven-page splurge on republican activist Mairead Farrell some months before the SAS gunned her down in Gibraltar.

Most of all, people bought *Magill* because of its spellbinding knack for putting public representatives in the dock and disecting them with the relish of a scalpel-wielding Jesuit. The former heckler in the stalls was now a major player. For example, the October '86 edition hardly exaggerated when it claimed credit for "The dismissal of Minister Of State, Eddie Collins, arising from an investigation by Fintan O'Toole". To borrow a phrase previously used by Collins in a Waterford speech, it was "a fine vindication" of the magazine's punching power.

In 1986 *Magill* was claiming 235,000 readers per issue. By early 1990 the party was rapidly fizzling out. Browne's crop of inspired youngsters had taken their probing minds to a national media determined to steal *Magill*'s clothes - the ones that fitted, anyway. Many of the advertisers had jumped ship. The last issue hit the shelves in July 1990. It resembled the Marie Celeste. The table was laid, the knives were out (Headline: FG IS DYING OF BOREDOM UNDER THE LEADERSHIP OF ALAN DUKES), but the crew had vanished. *Magill* was becalmed in a doldrums of lite entertainment (Prince, Jack's Army, the GAA) and advertorial goo (six pages on why Direct Marketing is fab).

So *Magill* went to Davy Jones Locker, but there was buried treasure yet to be recovered. Long after the magazine's demise a successful court application established that the short-lived *Magill TV Guide* should have been given access to RTE programme listings. Unfairly deprived of these, the publication never had a sporting chance of loosening the *RTE Guide*'s stranglehold on the market. Compensation was due.

In the summer of 1997 Vincent Browne resurrected *Magill*. The crusade continues...

PEOPLE WILL GET DRUNK

A Pocket Of Turbulence Over The Atlantic 1995

"Travel," wrote Mark Twain, "is fatal to prejudice, bigotry and narrow-mindedness." At Christmas 1995, an expedition from the travelling community went to extraordinary lengths to prove the great man wrong. Eighteen members of the Connors, Cash and Purcell families were embarking on the winter break of a lifetime, a trip to Disneyland in sunny California. Travelling on Irish and British passports, the tourists set off from London's Gatwick Airport in high spirits.

Shortly after the Northwest Airlines flight passed its point of no return, so did the behaviour of its Disney-bound consignment. Thirty thousand feet above the choppy Atlantic, members of the traveller families developed a drink problem. The problem was that the flight attendants had called closing time. The Connors, Cashs and Purcells were politely told that they'd had enough. Some of the travellers begged to differ. When this proved ineffectual, some felt they had no option but to borrow or steal. Young children were dispatched down the aisle, "Fagan-style", on an undercover mission to liberate shorts from the service trollies. The vigilent flight attendants repulsed their advances. The plane people of Ireland, and her sister island, stood up for their rights. The captain was summonsed from his cockpit to tell them to sit down again. He beat a hasty retreat when the pocket of on-board turbulence turned out to be unexpectedly severe.

As the shouting and swearing escalated, some of the travellers discovered a practical use for airplane food. A portion of potato, for instance, could be easily converted into a crude but effective spud missile. Some of the travellers implemented a boycott of the toilet facilities, leading to eye-witness reports that brought vividly to mind the words "slash" and "seats" in a novel setting. "The seating area was soiled," said a shocked airline official, Doug Killian, "people were urinating by their seats." A teenage boy had to intercede on his mother's side when a bout of fisticuffs broke out between his parents. The final, unforgivable, affront to the American Way was perpertrated by a number of miscreants who lit up cigarettes on the non-smoking flight.

A male flight attendant decided to fight fire with fire. The holiday makers soon had him rolling in the aisle. As chance would have it, several members of the United States Olympic Wrestling team were on the flight. The wrestlers moved in and subdued the troublemakers. The worst offenders arrived in the States handcuffed to their seats. The eighteen travellers never got within a thousand miles of the theme park of their dreams. They were hauled off the airplane in Minneapolis. One of the party, Michael Purcell, was carted away by the FBI. The others were held pending deportation on the next available departure for London. In-flight drinks would not be served.

The deportees were furious. They felt that the airline was clearly culpable of igniting the mayhem. Eileen Cash, one of the group's elders, told it like it was: "Northwest Airlines gave us drink on the plane, they shouldn't have. We were going on holiday and something happened on the plane. We feel ashamed and embarrassed over it, but we never did anything." Her daughter, Eileen Connors, added, "We are embarrassed by what happened. The man arrested was nothing to do with us. We were all separate. We were just a bit noisy. We never did anything." The man arrested for assault and intimidation, Michael Purcell, didn't exactly have "nothing to do" with Eileen Connors, as she claimed. He was Eileen Cash's son-in-law. She was Eileen Cash's daughter. What Eileen Connors meant to say, perhaps, was that she was not her brother-in-law-in-custody's keeper.

Anyway, Eileen Connors wanted the blame redirected at the real villians of the piece, Northwest Airlines. "My little girl, Eileen, who is three," said Eileen, "was punched on the back by an air hostess. The children were very disappointed, it was a Christmas holiday. They gave us a lot of drink. Why were they giving out drink? People will get drunk, people are not used to drinking shorts."

Meanwhile, the deportees turned their thoughts to Michael Purcell, still pondering the error of his ways in a Minneapolis clink. When Michael got home he would face a stern reminder that violence is never the answer. "All the family are going to kick up over this," said the man's irate mother-in-law. "He'll get some hiding".

A MIDNIGHT SWOOP ON A CONGESTED AREA

The Legion Of Mary Vs. Monto 1922-25

It was quite by chance that Frank Duff got into the business of resurrecting fallen women. The thirtysomething civil servant founded the Legion Of Mary in 1921 to make the world a better place. At first, the organization mainly ministered to the needs of the elderly patients of James's Street Hospital in Dublin's Liberties. One day in 1922 Duff set out to visit an invalid at No. 24 Chancery Lane. By mistake he called on No. 25. There, he encountered his first streetwalkers. And a sad, scrawny lot they were too. Duff saw a gap for a new saving scheme.

Frank Duff dispatched a brace of his priestly lieutenants around to No. 25. The clerics asked the prostitutes lodging there to mend their ways. The young girls said they'd like nothing better, but how would they put food on the table? Do the done thing, said the priests, and enter one of the Magdalen Asylums. These nun-run sweatshops dotted around the country provided harsh internal exile for women afflicted with social leprosy. No thanks, said the girls. They'd rather take their chances on the street. As a last resort, the Legionnaires offered to cover the prostitutes' weekly rent bill, a hefty £28, if they'd promise to mend their wicked ways.

Duff convened a meeting to discuss the plight of the girls at No. 25. It was decided that the first step on the road to redemption should be an intensive bombardment of prayer. All that was now needed was somewhere to hold the retreat. The capital's religious institutions didn't want to know. Struck by this deficit of Christian spirit, the Sisters Of Charity in Baldoyle pitched in with the offer of a vacant classroom. One of the few girls who opted out of the retreat went by the name of Honor Bright. She stayed on the game and met a grisly end in the Dublin mountains three years later. There was sufficient evidence to bring a Garda Superintendent and a doctor to court. They got off.

Frank Duff made his case to William T. Cosgrave, *de facto* Taoiseach of the new Free State government. Impressed, Cosgrave gave the Legion a big house on Harcourt Street, cost-free. The reformed prostitutes moved into the building, now christened the Sancta Maria Hostel. Duff extended his clean-up operation across Dublin's Southside, but his sights were set on the Northside's notorious red light district, Monto.

Monto was part of the scenery, albeit a part that was most clearly seen with the perspective of distance. Only eleven years earlier, the *Encyclopaedia Britannica* had marvelled at how Dublin's roaring skin-trade was "carried on more publicly than even in the south of Europe or Algeria". That writer lacked the practised blind eye of the city's denizens. A new police chief had implemented a zero tolerance policy some years before. His strategy of surprise raids and incessant harassment fell victim to its own success. Some brothels shut down, but the bulk of the displaced street-walkers promptly moved their operations to the front of the General Post Office. Upright citizens were scandalised by the flagrancy, not to mention the overpowering fragrance, of this display. Zero tolerance was quietly shelved and Monto got back to business as usual.

At its peak Monto covered a quarter square mile of buildings adjacent to the capital's main thoroughfare, Sackville Street. At the start of the Nineteenth Century thousands of British troops were billeted there in readiness for a Napoleonic invasion that never came. They, in turn, were sought out by young women who specialised in treating old war wounds and sports injuries. Eventually an elaborate three-tier system prevailed, with different classes of brothel servicing the needs of blue-ribband, white-collar and no-collar clients. Men of good reputation - including the future King Edward VII - entered the pricy Flash Houses through secret underground tunnels. Religious pictures decked the walls of the shantier establishments.

Monto mushroomed into a carnal Klondike by the malodorous Liffey. Business really boomed around the Dublin Horse Show, major Gaelic games finals and big race meetings. Alcohol sales generated more income than prostitution, a reasonable statistic when some establishments charged up to twenty times the normal bar price. Many premises operated a student discount scheme in the hopes of inculcating the bad habits of a lifetime.

The big losers were the prostitutes. They handed over two-thirds of their earnings to their Madams. They were frequently in hock to moneylenders for the clothes on their back. Disease was an occupational hazard. The bouncers attached to each brothel weren't just for unruly clients. They administered whatever beatings were deemed prudent to keep the girls compliant and profitable.

The Legion held several tactical talks. There was no shortage of discouraging advice. Duff was told that his street missionaries would be risking life and limb. He was warned he could be set up by prostitutes and blackmailed. The truth was, respectable Dublin had little enthusiasm for Duff's proposed do-gooding. Monto existed in a separate, parallel universe. Its presence wasn't regarded as a fit subject to be addressed from any pulpit. The civic authorities connived in this grand delusion. By coincidence, some members of Dublin Corporation collected very lucrative rents from the brothels.

Duff pressed on regardless. In March 1923 he led a band of associates into the heart of Monto in search of a sick girl they'd been told about. The girl was removed to hospital where she eventually died of advanced venereal disease. The ease of the rescue encouraged the Legionaries to go straight back for more. On that first day alone, they signed up forty girls for a retreat at the Sancta Maria Hostel. The Legion Of Mary visited Monto twice a week after that. In under two years, Duff was able to claim that there were only forty practising prostitutes left in the area. He'd even initiated a resettlement scheme, planting ordinary decent folk in the vacated brothels.

The Jesuits weighed in behind the Legion in the spring of 1925, breaking the Church's vow of silence on the subject of Monto. The order were holding their Lenten mission in the Pro-Cathedral, on the margin of the whore zone. On a February Sunday, the red light district was denounced from the Pro-Cathedral pulpit for the first time in living memory. Duff prepared for the main offensive. The next day, he led a big march into Monto, extracting promises from the Madams that they'd quit the area. The marchers swept all before them except for two tenacious proprietors. At first, the pair said they'd go if the Legion paid off assorted debts of £75. Then they changed their minds and demanded £1,500 to secure their departure. It was a move they would soon regret.

Duff went straight to Dublin Castle and explained his predicament to the Chief Commissioner of Police. Thirty hours later, on the night of March 12th, 1925, a large task force swept into the area. The cacophony of gunfire, screaming and street scuffles roused sleepers for miles, and when the racket finally subsided 120 fresh arrests were squashed into the city's police cells. The rumour-mill went into overdrive. Everybody who was anybody was reputed to be snared. In the event, an unnamed Donegal TD turned out to be the only notary caught in the web. Like just about everyone else arrested, he claimed that his sole purpose in Monto had been an after-hours tipple.

From the remove of Cork, the *Examiner* could say "No citizen of Dublin will need to be told why a wholesale police raid was carried out", and no citizen of Dublin was told. The *Irish Independent*'s coded report told of "a midnight swoop on a congested district in the northern area." The *Irish Times* simply ignored the biggest civil disturbance of the year, devoting its lead story instead to the number of spoilt votes in the recent by-elections. Ditto the *Evening Herald*, which instead devoted much of its front page to a report headlined "CLOCKS AND COWS". A pressing debate was underway in the British House Of Commons as to whether the introduction of Summer Time would confuse the nation's cattle.

The only people charged in the wake of the raid were the two Madams. One was sentenced to three months imprisonment, the other got off on a technicality. The mopping-up operation was consolidated with a large procession through Monto. Each abandoned brothel was individually blessed and a holy picture nailed to the door. In the space of three years, Frank Duff had achieved a stunning victory over squalor, sin and official sloth. He'd shamed church and state into confronting the demons on their doorstep.

Ireland's home-style prohibition era had begun. Within a few more years the Free State had clamped down on liquor sales and banned contraceptives, better known in official cant as "instruments of race suicide". By 1929 a catch-all Censorship Of Publications Act was in place, and by the following year every last nude had been stripped from Dublin's Municipal Gallery.

Decades later, the English poet Donald Davie paid testament to the work begun by Duff and taken up with gusto by the new State. "What I have always liked about the Irish Republic," reflected Davie, "is that it is, of all the societies that I know, the least 'sexy'."

THIS KIND OF NEAR THE BORDERLINE ACTIVITY WON'T DO

The Bishop And The Nightie 1966

When it first went on the air in the summer of 1962, the premise behind the "The Late Late Show" was to draw the viewers in for a traditional fireside evening, with Gay Byrne glad-handling guests and passing around the sandwiches. Everything went swimmingly until the beginning of 1966, when sparks started flying from the fireplace. In January a potentially lethal belt of the crozier was averted when the programme hastily withdrew its invitation to Victor Lownes, a Playboy executive visiting Ireland. In the run-up to his scheduled appearance, Lownes had told the press he was on a recruiting drive to snare Irish bunnies for pagan England's Playboy clubs. Not on the national broadcasting service, he wasn't.

The following month the Late Late aped the popular "Mrs. & Mrs." game which playfully illuminated the quirks and foibles of married life. It was quickly apparent that the Foxes from Terenure in Dublin were no swingers. Asked to pick a dream date from A, B or C, Mrs. Fox thought her hubby would most like to treat her to a night in the pub with the lads. Thoughtfully, he selected the romantic dinner for two. Mr. Fox was asked whether his wife would prefer a holiday in Spain, a Shannon cruise or a fortnight in New York. He correctly guessed the homebird option. At this point, the prospects of the item igniting into front-page scandal seemed slim.

The tremors began when Gaybo asked Mr. Fox the colour of his wife's nightdress on their wedding night. "Transparent", he said. Much tittering ensued. She was brought back into the studio and asked the same question. "For heaven's sake," clucked Gaybo, "watch every word you say." "I didn't wear any," said Mrs. Fox. When the laughter subsided she changed her answer to "white". That night three people phoned Montrose to complain that the nightie material clashed with the nation's moral fabric. There was a single telegram. It read: "Disgusted with disgraceful performance." The sender was the Bishop of Clonfert, Thomas Ryan.

The next day Bishop Ryan let fly from the pulpit. The show

had been "objectionable", "debasing" and "disgraceful". The bishop thundered: "Surely, if we want to look at television, we are entitled to see a programme that is more in keeping with moral standards traditional in our Catholic country." He called on all "decent Irish Catholics" to protest. Mrs. Fox declined to comment, except to say the fuss was "too ridiculous for words". Gaybo declared himself "absolutely at a loss to know why there should be any objection by anyone". The lead editorial in the *Irish Times* scolded: "his Lordship is killing a fly with a sledgehammer". The *Times* gave Gaybo its endorsement. The presenter was, it said, "Irish, of the Irish, accomplished and bland".

Having said he couldn't see what the bishop's problem was, Gay was pushed into submitting a ritual apology. The item, he now accepted, "was embarrassing to a section of viewers". Bishop Ryan twisted the knife. He'd make no comment on Byrne's apology, but he could say that the Director General of Telefís Eireann, Kevin McCourt, had phoned him personally with an explanation he'd deemed satisfactory. A Montrose spokesman said the Authority had "no knowledge" of any such communication.

The Bishop had called it wrong. The general public was not outraged. In fact, the general public wasn't particularly interested. On the day after Bishop Ryan's outburst Telefís Eireann received a modest sixty calls on the subject, and thirty-six of those were in support of the item. Individuals writing to the press seemed bent on perpetrating lame jokes about "The Late Night Shift" and "The Late Late Nightie Show". Trinity students announced a march down O'Connell Street in protest against the Bishop's "absurdity" and Gaybo's "fawning apology". The marchers would be dressed in white nighties. The modernising mohair men in government saw no percentage in getting involved and kept schtum.

As the *Irish Times* editorial had correctly surmised, the bishop had rashly left himself out on a limb. In the newspaper's words: "A lapse of taste has been treated as if it were an outrage to morals." Knee-jerk reaction fell to the middle ranks of the Establishment who felt that, whatever the situation's merits, a Bishop shouldn't be ignored.

Loughrea Town Commission weighed in with a motion that

the Late Late was "a dirty programme that should be abolished altogether". Members of the Mayo GAA Board condemned it, before further discussion of the matter was ruled out of order. Meath Vocational Education Committee passed a resolution generally deploring the Late Late on the grounds of its mediocracy and low morals. Worse, the programme was "anti-national". When Mr. P. Cahill of Waterford County Council proposed a motion congratulating Telefis Eireann for "a good show", the Chairman replied "I don't think we should go that far" and declared the subject closed.

Senator J.B. O'Quigley reminded the Seanad that this "deplorable" fare was being funded by taxpayers' money. He stated, "This kind of near the borderline activity won't do". Senator Sheehy Skeffington blamed the education system for failing the country. Because a significant proportion of the Irish were "an under-educated people" it came as no surprise that "vulgarity" topped the viewing figures. Senator C.B. McDonald objected that far too often the Late Late's guests and panellists seemed primed with "one too many over the mark". The only TD to speak out, Stephen Barrett, hoped that "with the passage of time Mr. Gay Byrne's mind will become more enlightened".

The deputy was to be severely disappointed. Within a few weeks, a Late Late panellist would call the Bishop Of Galway "a moron". The Swinging Sixties had arrived, Irish style.

I'M GOING TO FUCKING HAVE YOU BABY

Eamon Dunphy Vs. Official Ireland

Eamon Dunphy Vs. Official Ireland has more than a whiff of Frankenstein about it: vexed by the perfidy of the world and the veniality of its creator, the creature wreaks a terrible vengeance.

There were two versions of Official Ireland when Dunphy was growing up in Fifties Drumcondra. One was the mythical one of happy maidens and simple piety. The other one involved knuckling down, keeping up appearances, raising twelve kids and not thinking too much about the country being banjaxed. Little Eamon didn't subscribe to either.

To the young Dunphy the faces presented by Official Ireland seemed unsympathetic. He didn't appreciate being "fondled" by a priest, or Dublin Corporation's strenuous efforts to evict his family. His patched clothes and empty pockets marked him as an outsider in a well-to-do neighbourhood. His father's hatred for all-powerful Fianna Fail stamped an imprimatur on Eamon's suspicion of authority. Lack of funds forced him to leave school by fourteen. At fifteen he signed for Manchester United as an apprentice, showing a clean pair of heels to the Dublin store where he toiled as a messenger boy.

His first encounter with Irish officialdom had a bruising effect on the nineteen-year-old. Ireland were playing Spain in a crucial tiebreak for the 1966 World Cup Finals. The expectation amongst many of the players was that the match would be in London, where the team could rely on a good turn-out of support. Instead, the Irish Association and their Spanish counterparts somehow engineered a fixture in distant and disinterested Paris. It was young Dunphy's Irish debut. He didn't anticipate that the night before the match the team officials would prime their players with copious pints and a visit to a whorehouse. Ireland lost 1-0. Much later he reflected, "It was then that I realised that if you don't have leadership and you don't have values, you've got nothing."

Manchester United didn't work out. Dunphy's playing career was spent in the English lower divisions with also-rans like

Millwall, Charlton and Reading. Before returning to Ireland in the late Seventies, Dunphy took a withering revenge on the corrupt feudal world of professional football by writing the first worthwhile soccer book, "Only A Game". His literary debut was borne out of a diary he'd kept during his last season at Milwall, "because I wanted to explore the process of failure." After finishing his playing days back in Dublin with Shamrock Rovers, he was offered a sports column with the *Sunday World*. Vincent Browne then attempted to sign him for *Magill* magazine, but only on the condition that Browne would ghost-write his stuff. Dunphy graceously declined. On Browne's recommendation, the new *Sunday Tribune* took him on board. Cosy consensus got an elbow in the face.

Perhaps it was his long years abroad, but everywhere he looked Eamon Dunphy saw things that the natives couldn't or wouldn't face up to. To him it was abundantly clear that the Emperors of Irish sport had no clothes. And boy, were some of them under-endowed. Irish manager Eoin Hand and the FAI "decent-skins" were uninspired jobsworths. Our Greatest Living Player, Liam Brady, was a preening dilettante. New man Jack Charlton was a blinkered bully.

The sharpness of Dunphy's game was lost on Jack's Army, a generation of football fans whose idea of nirvana was a 1-0 win (a deflected toe-poke from a corner), fifteen pints, a furtive grope and a batter-burger. Dunphy Vs. Charlton reached mock-epic proportions, with the public firmly behind the Geordie. Big Jack suggested he'd like to punch out Eamon's lights, so Dunphy donned a false beard and shades and sat in on a Charlton pub talk. Before long, Charlton fell back behind a defensive wall: "He's gone. I don't want to acknowledge him. I don't want to know about Dunphy."

The Plain People Of Ireland Vs. Eamon Dunphy came to an unsavoury head after he was misrepresented as saying he was ashamed to be Irish. He recalled how, leaving Dublin Airport, "One woman called me and took a photograph. I was smiling... As soon as she'd taken the photo she said 'Ya fuckin' bastard!'." That evening climaxed with a group of supporters drumming up a rousing version of "You'll never beat the Irish". On his car, with him inside.

The football stuff soon wrote itself - good players, bad manager, Neanderthal tactics, end of story. Restless, he began firing off slingshots at sleepy semi-states, the Loopy Left and whatever else didn't take his fancy. Michael D. Higgins rose to the bait early on, characterising Dunphy as a cheap and derivative "Mary Kenny without the charlady towel on her head." Much later - after Dunphy took the plunge and questioned Michelle Smith's shock Olympic haul - the swimmer's wounded father branded the controversialist "a failed footballer, a failed journalist... a failed human being" who built success "on the back of insulting all our national heroes". It was the familiar, bankrupt mantra of the Olé brigade.

Much as Dunphy tries to represent his attacks on Official Ireland as a principled crusade against complacency and dishonesty, things just seem to keep getting real personal. Partly this has to do with Ireland being a small place, partly it's to do with Dunphy's addictive use of charged language. On U2, for example: "They fucked me." John Waters, meanwhile, he deemed "a little bollox" and "a gobshite". Gay Byrne he described as a "gone, sad, pathetic figure". Vincent Browne was simply "power crazy". Oh, and people who ring in to radio talk shows should have better things to do with their time.

In Dublin's High Court, in 1997, Dunphy was asked: "Is it true you once phoned Fintan O'Toole and told him to watch his back, that you were going to break his 'fucking legs'?" No, he answered, he'd said something entirely different. What he did say to the *Irish Times'* journalist was: "Fintan, I'm going to fucking have you, baby. Watch the back page next Sunday." The remarks were made after O'Toole had written an article about Dunphy's baliwick, the *Sunday Independent.* Dunphy wanted to register his displeasure with the piece. O'Toole's response was, "Don't threaten me." To which Eamon replied, "I'm not. I'm promising you." In court, Dunphy dismissed the exchange as a case of "petty bitching". For the record, the High Court heard Dunphy describe Fintan O'Toole as a "considerable gentleman" whom he admired. Jack Charlton was a decent man whom he liked. And "gone, sad, pathetic" Gay Byrne? "I love Mr. Gay Byrne," he told the court. "He is one of the great people in this country."

This remarkable capacity to lavish harsh words on individuals he holds in the highest esteem hasn't earned Eamon Dunphy the universal love and admiration of his peers. John Hume, Mary Robinson, John Waters, Sinead O'Connor, Joe O'Connor, Roddy Doyle, Seamus Heany, Dick Spring, Michael D. Higgins, Prionsias De Rossa and Pat Kenny head up a long list of luminaries who've felt the business end of his pen. Several have responded with legal proceedings.

Many would suggest that if Dunphy took the time to look down, he'd see that the high moral ground he declaims from is actually a tottering scaffolding of creaking soapboxes. He'd doubtless prefer to be regarded in the light of his own hero, Sir Matt Busby, about whom he has said: "He used his qualities of ruthlessness for what he perceived to be the common good."

Either way, no Irish good feud guide would be complete without Eamon Dunphy.

THEY'RE A PACK OF FOREIGNERS

The Rise And Fall Of Catholic Marxism 1968

It was 1968. The forces of change, icebound throughout the De Valera decades, were beginning to thaw. But the warming winds weren't from hippy-dippy San Francisco or Swinging pagan London. Ireland's stiff collars were being tickled by a balmy Mediterranean breeze.

Since 1963 the Second Vatican Council had been doing for the Catholic Church what The Beatles were doing for youth culture. A Church defined along hard lines from time immemorial suddenly began to mellow out. Previously forbidden books flooded the seminaries. Fresh ideas began to circulate. Young priests began to experiment with mind-expanding notions.

The faithful weren't long in noticing the sea-change. For generations, the function of the parish priest had been to buttress the existing social order and obsess about sex. It was no accident that working class priests and nuns tended to get shunted abroad to the missions while their middle-class brethren were accommodated within the domestic scheme of things. But now, strange new concerns wafted down from the pulpits, about poverty and social justice on our own doorsteps. Even ecumenism, until recently tantamount to heavy-petting with the Devil, was given a tentative embrace.

Then, in July 1968, Pope Paul VI threw a wobbler and jammed on the brakes. *Humanae Vitae* stopped the modernisers in their tracks. Artificial contraception, it stated, was a ticket to Hell. This didn't go down so well with those Catholics already using birth control in the belief that it was cool with the new laid-back Church. Traditionalists rejoiced - the tinkering trendies in Rome had been mucking with their minds for too long. But the genie was already out of the bottle. Liberation theology had established a toehold in Ireland. The Pray-In was born.

The Pray-In was the brainchild of a band of ecumenicists who were quickly tagged Catholic Marxists. The antics they provoked didn't recall Karl so much as Groucho, Harpo and Chico. In July 1968 the group produced a magazine, *Grille*, to encourage the open dialogue that the Pope was now trying to suffocate. The first Pray-In was scheduled for an August Sunday afternoon in St. Andrews Church, Westland Row, central Dublin. A sizeable press corps turned up expecting a holy show. They weren't disappointed.

A group of perhaps fifty worshipers from the *Grille* camp entered the church and assembled in a small alcove. The Blessed Sacrament had been removed by Church authorities after the final mass of that morning, in anticipation of "disrespectful" scenes. As the *Grille* contingent prepared to pray, a hostile crowd of parishioners assembled around them. After a few opening prayers, *Grille*'s John Feeney rose and spoke some words of welcome. He then started reading from the Bible.

This incensed the gathered locals who knew that good Catholics did not read the Bible - that was the clergy's job. A middle-aged man sprang from the mob of parishioners and launched himself at Feeney, knocking his Good Book to the ground. Another *Grille* disciple, John Byrne, immediately took up the reading. At this point a woman collared the attacker and dragged him away from his victim. It was the man's wife. "You're making a show of yourself," she chided. "Let them go on with it. It'll all fizzle out."

It didn't fizzle out just yet. No sooner was the first assailant led away than a force of parish vigilantes waded into the ranks of the prayer-group "pushing them about, throwing punches and pulling women's headscarves off". John Byrne's response was to strike up a hymn. Unfortunately, if music be the food of love the irate locals were on a strict diet. Byrne was unceremoniously silenced with a fist in the teeth.

The belligerent parishioners hurled rhetorical questions at the strangers invading their space. "Are you a Catholic?" they called. "Are you Irish?" "Are you from this parish?" "Are you a Communist?" "Why don't you go and pray in your own church?" In fact, the Christian Marxists had attempted without success to get permission to hold their Love-In in a number of churches. Amid taunts of "sacrilege!" John Feeney signalled the retreat. He told his battered crew that they would complete their Pray-In at the University Church on Stephen's Green a short distance away.

As they left the church, the pioneers of Catholic Marxism were jeered and heckled. One man, a devotee of the Latin liturgy, wanted to know, "If you're Catholics why were you reading in English?" Another foot-soldier on a crusade from Ringsend insisted, "If this happened in our parish, we'd get them by the scruff of the neck and throw them out. Look at their faces, they're not Irishmen at all. They're a pack of foreigners." A squad of Gardai had been assigned to oversee the Pray-In. They loitered with no intent of intervening.

A former Trappist monk and schoolteacher by the name of Louis Mulderry told reporters that the eviction was a victory for the common man. He said, "The men who acted against these people look on them as a lot of snooty would-be intellectuals trying to take over their parish." Shortly afterwards, over at University Church, John Feeney stood beneath the pulpit and began to read from the Bible. A man approached him. It was the former monk again, anxious to save another parish from snooty would-be intellectualism. He handed Feeney a note. Feeney read it aloud. It said: "This church has been booked for a private christening. Can't you show some respect for the church, and the sacraments?"

In deference, the *Grille* refugees switched to silent prayer. The tranquillity of the scene was disturbed only by the incessant wailing of a waterlogged infant at the other end of the church. John Feeney then concluded the Pray-In by registering the group's displeasure with the Pope's birth control encyclical, the Soviet tanks in Prague and the religious folk who'd beaten them up an hour earlier.

As the Catholic Marxists spilled out onto the street they were confronted by more opponents. Amused Gardai stood by as the two wings of mainstream piety jostled each other for over an hour. The Gardai had less cause to be smug shortly afterwards when the *Grille* organization mounted a protest outside the Garda Club to protest against the visit of a group of Chicago police to Dublin. The picket was "in penance for the activities of Irish Americans generally." *Grille* explained: "These people are not noted for any great concern on Christian issues in the USA, such as Vietnam and race relations."

It was a bad call. The protest's profound lack of impact simply demonstrated that nobody really gave a toss about the Catholic Marxists, just so long they kept out of other people's churches. Dublin's Archbishop McQuaid signed off the brief summer of Catholic Marxism by restating the church's free-market position on social issues. "No measures of social security," he proclaimed, "can eliminate human poverty". Many of the country's poorest citizens slept tighter in their beds that night.

ONLY MESSING

Tony Murphy Vs. The Hare Krishnas 1987

It was a three day wonder, but for that short duration 25-year-old Tony Murphy from Rathfarnham in Dublin was the most talked about man in Ireland. There was plenty to talk about, including abduction, captivity in a remote hideaway, indoctrination, and a climactic daredevil escape. What really caught the public's imagination, though, was the drugged ice cream.

It was September 1987. Murphy, a former supermarket worker, had been on the missing persons list for over a week when he reappeared with a sinister and shocking tale. His story began with a visit to the Hare Krishna restaurant on Crow Street in central Dublin. There he hoped to alleviate a temporary cash-flow problem by raising a few bob. The kindly Hare Krishnas didn't give him money, but they treated him to some edifying vegetarian fare and an ice cream dessert. Drugged ice cream, Tony later surmised. He blanked out.

His next memory was of being in a different room where he was offered more food. Perhaps surprisingly, in the light of how his last snack had disagreed with him, he ate it. Next thing he knew he was on an island, which he learned was Inisrath, on Upper Loch Erne in Co. Fermanagh. In all, he spent eleven days there. Tony repeatedly pleaded for his liberty, he said, but he was told that Krishna was anxious for him to stay. Apparently it was also Krishna's will that he'd be given a few thumps and locked up.

During his time on the island, Tony received a neck injury which necessitated a visit to Enniskillen General Hospital. He attributed this injury to a pair of roughneck acolytes who accosted him in a bid to shave his head against his will. Another version of events later emerged, that he'd been hurt during a bout of playful wrestling. No matter, at least the hospital visit would put an end to his ordeal. Wouldn't it? Incredibly, no. He didn't breathe a word of his predicament to the medical staff because he feared they were "in cahoots" with the Hare Krishnas. So he meekly returned to his island captivity.

But Tony Murphy did escape, in a style befitting James Bond.

He climbed out of a window, shinned down a pillar, navigated a leaky boat, stole a car (which, as fate would have it, belonged to a Hare Krishna) and headed south for the border. Eventually he found refuge at a Monaghan Garda station. Reunited with his parents, he went to Rathfarnham Garda Station to declare that he was no longer a missing person. He told Gardai that he didn't want to press any charges, nor did he want his adventure publicised.

But Tony's parents weren't going to take their son's kidnapping lying down. They insisted he tell everything to his parish priest, Fr. Paul Murphy. Fr. Murphy arranged for Tony to be interviewed on RTE Radio 1's "Liveline" programme. Tony related his story to the listening nation. A Hare Krishna spokesman, Shaunaka Ram Das, denounced the whole tale as a pack of lies. He said that Murphy had come to the island voluntarily and had later concocted a Baron Munchausen-scale fantasy to mollify his concerned parents.

The saga would occupy a second "Liveline" programme, and then a third. Tony's sordid saga came as no surprise to many callers, who had always suspected so much. The words "cult" and "brainwashing" were much bandied about. Besides, any group who could do that to an innocent ice cream clearly possessed a limitless capacity for evil. On the second programme Fr. Murphy said he knew nothing about the ways of the Hare Krishnas but it seemed obvious that Tony Murphy was telling the truth. Then came the bombshell. A famous Monty Python punchline reverberated across the land. The one that goes: "At this point my argument falls totally to the ground."

Tony Murphy's whereabouts on the day he claimed he'd first gone "missing" were no longer a mystery. He'd been on the telly. An RTE crew had filmed him demonstrating outside the Russian embassy in support of imprisoned Soviet Hare Krishnas. The *Irish Press* also had photos of him there. In fact, Murphy was holding aloft the main banner at the assembly. This revelation pushed the drugged ice cream scenario back to the top of the agenda for a third "Liveline" running. Rather than accept that Murphy had led everyone a merry dance, diehard callers argued that his amnesia simply proved he'd been acting under the influence. The harassed

Hare Krishnas eventually got their wish and the Gardai launched an official investigation.

Tony Murphy's statement took three days to complete and ran to thirty-three pages. Investigations revealed that Murphy had previously told friends he'd been involved in the murder of a man in the Dublin Mountains. A detective questioned him about this. He said he was "only messing". Officers told Murphy that if he brought the Krishnas to court on kidnap charges, he would land himself in trouble. He brought them anyway, telling the judge that to recant now would be "unfair" to other potential victims.

Judge Gerard Buchanan dismissed Murphy's allegations as "outrageous". The blanket of unsubstantiated coverage they'd received was a regrettable case of "trial by media". After the judge delivered his verdict, Hare Krishna spokesman Shaunaka Rishi Das gave his. He stated grimly, "The involvement of the Catholic clergy in this case merits further investigation."

The end of the line for Tony Murphy's bogus journey was a three-year suspended sentence for wasting Garda time.

THIS IS SPORT, NOT WAR

The Irish Soccer Experience 1920-94

When sport and sectarian politics mix-it in Ireland, time and again the Beautiful Game has been horribly disfigured in the crossfire. Rugby Union, each contest a game of two Haves, stayed held together by its supporting caste. The GAA accommodated the Have Nots, but flourished behind a different kind of exclusivity. Croke Park HQ never needed to legislate for crunch ties between Loyalist and Nationalist hurling teams, or breakaways by that part of the GAA which regards itself as inalienably British. Pursuits like canoeing, badminton and pigeon-fancying admit limited scope for fomenting mob hatred. The devotion of the urban working-class was both soccer's great strength and its fatal weakness.

The Irish Football Association was born and reared in Belfast. Between 1880 and 1920, Dublin barely got a look-in when it came to staging international matches. The capital, being the capital, resented playing second city. The 1920 Irish Cup Semi-Finals were the prologue to a bitter divorce.

That year Glentoran, with a support base in the staunchly Loyalist Harland & Wolff shipyards, met rabidly nationalist Belfast Celtic. The match finished a draw. The replay was at Cliftonville. Twelve minutes from the end, Celtic's Gowdy was sent off. This sparked a pitch invasion by the team's strident Sinn Fein following. In the ensuing riot, several civilians and police were shot and many hundreds injured. Remarkably, only two people were arrested. A man called Goodman was charged with possessing a gun. One Hugh McVitty, meanwhile, was done for "indecent behaviour".

The second Semi-Final fared little better. It was between Glenavon and Shelbourne. Glenavon travelled south to Dublin for the tie. For ninety minutes the home support hurled dog's abuse and missiles. The Northerners scurried off the pitch a beaten team. With Belfast Celtic expelled from the competition for the treasonable behaviour of their fans, Shelbourne lifted the Irish Cup for 1920 without the bother of playing in the Final.

The 1921 Semi-Finals once again brought Shelbourne face to face with Glenavon. Only this time the Northern team had home advantage. The War Of Independence was raging. Mayhem reigned. Routine headlines of the day included "EXECUTIONS IN CORK", "CLERGYMAN'S HOUSE BOMBED" and "LIVELINESS IN DUNDALK". The *Irish Times* carried a regular Deaths Pending column entitled "Courts-Martial Sentences". Shelbourne emerged from a fraught Belfast visit with a 0-0 result, sufficient to take Glenavon back to Dublin. At this juncture, the Belfast-based IFA put the boot in. Inexplicably, they ordered Shelbourne to return North for the replay.

The Dublin clubs rallied around their top team. The IFA decision was denounced as "unjust". The Protests And Appeals Committee was clearly partisan. The Dublin clubs wanted it disbanded. The IFA Chairman, Mr. Wilton, said the Association couldn't bow to interference from its Dublin contingent. "It was impossible now for them to undo what had been done," he insisted. At the same meeting, the Dublin officials sought clarification of a "flag incident" at a recent amateur international in Paris. Chairman Wilton explained that the mischievous French had made elaborate arrangements for the Irish players to parade onto the pitch behind an Irish flag. Over his dead body, he'd informed his hosts. He was sure that the Dublin "sportsmen" of the IFA would "deprecate" the introduction of politics into football.

That was the final straw. The divorce was finalised two months later, in May of 1921. Complaining that they were "smarting under an injustice", Shelbourne had already withdrawn from the Irish Cup. Now, the southern representatives split from the Irish League to form the 26-county Football Association of Ireland. The partitioning of Irish football virtually eliminated sectarian riots at club fixtures, with one glaring exception. Violence continued to dog Belfast Celtic, now virtually alone and friendless in a hostile jurisdiction. The club was eventually hounded out of existence in 1950.

Three decades after the split, the IFA and FAI could still dip into a common pool of players for international duty. The Southern association discouraged its squad members from turning out for the North, but international matches paid a handsome wage. With the players manfully resisting the FAI's appeals to boycott its Northern counterpart, a mysterious campaign of intimidation started up towards the end of the Forties. Anonymous threats were issued against collaborators. When the players showed no sign of caving in, the scare tactics were extended to their families and clubs. At the same time, the FAI was making crude attempts to demonise the IFA. The Dublin association repeatedly invited the Six County body to form a Joint Committee to administer the game on an All-Ireland basis. It was an offer they knew the IFA must refuse.

The Southern players eventually succumbed to the combination of official displeasure and orchestrated intimidation. In February 1950 Sean Fallon told the Northern Ireland association to include him out for their game against England. Many years later he admitted, "the pressure put on my family was too much." At the time, though, Fallon's announcement was heralded as an affirmation of faith and fatherland. One month later, on Saint Patrick's Day, Con Martin announced that he would no longer be taking the North's pieces of silver. A triumphal FAI congratulated him on his "spirited action". Seventeen other players announced a boycott of the IFA over the following days. "Many people consider this to be a very patriotic gesture," observed the *Irish Times*, "as an international appearance means £20 to a selected player." The newspaper pointed out, however, that the sacrifice being made by most of these patriots was roughly zilch, since the prospect of the North ever requesting their services was "rather slender".

Several times from the Fifties to the Seventies, the FAI and IFA trotted out various chat-up lines to each other. But neither was really interested in a relationship. For one, a unified Association would mean half the number of prestige posts. And anyway, Northern Ireland did very nicely without its erstwhile southern reinforcements. The British Home International Championship each Spring guaranteed glamour ties with England and Scotland, plus a run-out against Wales. Northern Ireland even mounted a respectable campaign in the 1958 World Cup Finals. Meanwhile, the Republic's famous capacity to laugh in the face of defeat made the team a great favourite across Europe. In 1973 an All-Ireland XI stretched Brazil as a curtain raiser to new North/South negotiations. The reconciliation process didn't last much past the final whistle. It was formally abandoned in 1978, the year that the two Irelands met for the first time.

That year, Northern Ireland and the Republic were drawn together in a qualifying round for the European Championships. The first meeting took place at Lansdowne Road late in '78. In the run-up to the match, the media implemented a policy of "Don't Mention The War". Coverage of the crunch tie was confined to team news and a quote from Johnny Giles. "This is sport," he sagely noted, "not war". Up to ten thousand Northern Ireland supporters alighted in the heart of Dublin. Gardai mounted a huge security operation, no spectator would be left un-frisked. Both teams dutifully conspired to dampen any excitement, producing a drab 0-0 draw.

Bored into submission, both sets of fans traipsed out of the ground. Everything had gone perfectly to plan. Under heavy Garda escort, the Northbound hordes made their way towards the train station. And then it all went horribly wrong. *Ars-en-all, ars-en-all*, an arsenal! The Gardai had confiscated anything that could possibly harm a fly, from flagpoles to pencils to fly-swatters. But nobody had thought to clear away the mounds of fist-sized stones lying around Lansdowne Rugby Club's newly built clubhouse. The rioting raged for hours.

The return tie in Windsor Park was set for November 1979, but before that, in September, Belfast's Linfield FC were drawn to face Dundalk in the UEFA Cup. It was a match made in Hell. Linfield's terrace chants were famous for their colourful, if anatomically dubious, homages to the Pope. The border town of Dundalk was regarded in the Linfield catchment area as a Provo El Paso. The first round would be played in Dundalk. Still, the Gardai had learned valuable lessons at Lansdowne Road the previous September.

In the event, the words "dog", "ate" and "homework" sprang vividly to mind. Five thousand Linfield fans found themselves at liberty to run riot on the terraces. A similar number of Dundalk fans were straining to pacify them with extreme prejudice. Several coachloads of Cliftonville supporters had followed their hated rivals Linfield south in the hope of seeing the North's footballing Goliath cut down to size.

RTE's radio coverage of the match was disrupted when broadcaster Philip Greene had to be rescued from his commentary box which was being dismantled by excited Linfield fans. The flow of play was somewhat spoiled by squads of riot police crossing the pitch. The last quarter of the match was played out before empty terraces vacated by fleeing Linfield supporters. As the Northern coaches left town, they shed a ballast of petrol bombs via the back windows. Their hosts reciprocated by lining the route out of town, hurling deadly missiles at the departing visitors.

The upshot of the match was a 1-1 draw and a fine of £870 on Dundalk "for insufficient security service". Europe's football authorities slapped a two match home ban on Linfield and ordered the club to pay for the damage to Dundalk's Oriel Park ground. Linfield's home leg against Dundalk would now take place in a continental country of Linfield's choosing. They picked Holland, spiritual home of all Orangemen. Dundalk FC released a statement, apparently with no humorous intent, insisting they were "confident that the good relationship between Dundalk and Linfield would continue."

Precisely the same sort of "good relationship" was in evidence weeks later when the Republic arrived in Belfast for their return tie with Northern Ireland. Lord Mountbatten's murder days before contributed to a poisonous atmosphere at Windsor Park. Tricolours were set ablaze on the terraces. The Republic midfielder Gerry Daly was carried off after a spectator attempted long-distance brain surgery on him with an unsterilized projectile. The visitors chased victory but goalkeeper Pat Jennings responded with goalmouth heroics. The North won by the game's only goal. The final whistle heralded a five year lull in cross-border football hostilities.

By 1984 the penny had finally dropped with the Irish authorities. Glasgow Rangers were coming to Dublin to face Bohemians at Dalymount Park in a UEFA Cup game. As sure as night followed day, Linfield fans would arrive in their thousands to pay homage to a club regarded as the Swiss Guard of Loyalism. The Gardai, club officials and British Embassy representatives drew up a thorough set of precautionary measures to prevent violence, including extra fencing and segregated entrances.

The Bohemians fans had drawn up their own precautionary measures to ensure that the visitors had no monopoly on thuggism. The home support burned Union Jacks, chanted IRA slogans and jibed their counterparts that they'd be going home in a fucking ambulance. The Battle Of Dalymount, as the newspapers dubbed it, haemorrhaged onto the surrounding streets. Four out of every five Glasgow Rangers fans charged at the Bridewell Jail that night were Northern Irish. A fleet of up to eighty Northbound coaches ran a gauntlet through hostile mobs at Finglas, Ashbourne, Drogheda and other centres. Many of those carried North were unwilling Scots fans who'd arrived by ferry from Liverpool. They'd been herded onto the coaches by Gardai. One officer told it like it was: "They'll all go to the North whether they like it or not.".

Nine years later, in November 1993, Windsor Park was the venue for the last fixture of Northern Ireland's qualifying campaign for the 1994 World Cup Finals. The North had already missed the boat for the USA next summer. Their visitors from down the road could still qualify if they got a result in Belfast and Spain nobbled Denmark in Seville. The handful of incognito Republic supporters dotted about the terraces fooled no-one. The smell of fear gave them away. Before the game Alan McLoughlin, one of Jack's Anglos, volunteered a footballing appraisal of the political situation. "There's been a lot of atrocities off the pitch," he said.

It was like Twelfth night in the pocket-size stadium, a serried sea of orange flags, red hands and Union Jacks. "The Sash" segued into "God Save The Queen" which rose to a crescendo of "No Surrender", and back into "The Sash". Derailing the Republic's bandwagon would be fair return from the qualifying campaign. The home fans applauded the visitors' high work-rate with cries of "Fenian scum", "Hello England's rejects" and "Bonner ye Taig bastard". With the match three-quarters done, Jimmy Quinn rewarded the faithful with a fierce volley past the Republic's goal-keeper. Windsor Park erupted with bellicose glee. As the roar subsided, a massed refrain welled up of "Always look on the bright side of life". Jack's heroes were drowning amid a wash of full throated Norn Irony.

The Republic's American Dream was minutes away from extinction when the lad McLoughlin made his second memorable contribution to a memorable day. His first goal for Ireland sucked the life out of Windsor Park. The deathly silence that fell on the ground went unheard in thousands of homes and pubs south of the border. In a post-match interview, the delirious McLoughlin completed an immortal hat-trick. Pulsating with emotion in the heart of Belfast, he told reporters, "I'm glad for the fans back in Ireland."

In changed circumstances, the Windsor Park faithful would have applauded the sentiment.

ARMCHAIR LIBERALS WHO SIT AT HOME CONDEMNING APARTHEID

Hostile Trendies Vs. Foster & Allen 1985

Poor old Foster & Allen. There they were, polishing the gold discs, just minding their own business. Then *whack!* They never saw it coming. The Trendies had been sniping at the popular Co. Westmeath duo for years but this was different, concerted, an all-out assault.

It was the Autumn of 1985. Life was good for Mick Foster (Favourite Film: The "Carry On" series) and Tony Allen (Unfulfilled Ambition: None). Conventional wisdom has it that a gentleman is someone who can play the accordion but doesn't. Neither Foster nor Allen had ever been cowed by convention. The pair were gearing up for another sell-out Irish tour. They had three albums sitting pretty in the UK charts. The world was their pearly oyster.

The spark that detonated the powderkeg that shattered the idyll was a simple letter. The Irish Anti-Apartheid Movement (IAAM) wrote to the duo pointing out that their visits to South Africa "provided great assistance" to that country's white supremacist junta. The IAAM cited The Chieftains, The Dubliners, Niall Tobin and other performers who had turned down lucrative offers to play Sun City.

There was nothing new in this. The IAAM had written to Foster & Allen before. The organisation's Chairman, Dr. Kader Asmal, told the press that two previous appeals to the duo had yielded no response. This was hardly surprising. Foster & Allen were of the old school of Irish entertainers who respected the fact that deals and ideals are like men and women - one isn't necessarily better than the other, they're just different.

Contacted at a Tralee hotel, a bemused Tony Allen pointed out that Foster & Allen had, in fact, no plans for going to South Africa. This was true. The previous week they had announced details of their forthcoming world tour and the Dark Continent didn't figure. In fact, they'd only returned from Sun City a few months previously, and nobody'd raised so much as an eyebrow.

But something had happened in those middling months of 1985. Something big. Pop music had found its Manifold Destiny at Live Aid. Righting a wrong was now more intrinsic to rock'n'roll than writing a song. At precisely the same time, South Africa was just coming to the boil as an issue in Ireland thanks largely to a spirited group of Dunnes Stores workers whose dogged efforts to keep South African fruit off the shelves gave the Anti-Apartheid cause ultra-high visibility.

As calls mounted for his resignation from the Seanad, Senator Donie Cassidy took the opportunity to point out that - contrary to a widely held belief - he was not the duo's manager. Meanwhile, Tony Allen spelled it out again - they had no plans to tour South Africa. Allen added that he "did not see any examples of Apartheid on previous visits to the country". That casual utterance set the musos alight with moral indignation.

But the fact remained that Foster & Allen had no plans to return to South Africa. That wasn't good enough. They must swear an oath never to go back. Written in blood would be nice.

This was payback time for the men waggishly dubbed Voerster & Outspan by the rock critic George Byrne. Their flouting of the cultural boycott was bad enough, but there was more. For years they'd converted maudlin tripe into multi-platinum success while musicians who were clearly their moral and artistic superiors struggled to command the attention of three drunks, a barman and a girlfriend who was getting too chatty with the guy on the sound-desk. Most of all though, it was time to settle the score for that infamous "Top Of The Pops" appearance when the duo had dishonoured their caste by pretending to be leprechauns.

"It's a disgrace", said Donal Lunny. "They're sacrificing their morals" reflected Those Nervous Animals. U2's Adam Clayton thought it was "absolutely clear why they shouldn't go". Dave Fanning employed the words "ignorant", "stupid" and "disgusting". Paul Brady, without saying exactly why, found it "very hard to believe that a senator in Ireland could be entirely stupid". Chris De Burgh refused to issue a blanket condemnation. Having played South Africa himself, he knew "more about the situation than 99% of the Armchair Liberals who sit at home condemning Apartheid." Gavin Friday devastated South Africa's huge Electro-Da Da fan-base with the news that he "wouldn't even allow a record of mine to be released there."

Predictably, Foster & Allen's show at Dublin's Stadium was disrupted by protesters. The audience cheered as the disruptive do-gooders were ejected. After that, there was little else either side could do. In the end, Foster & Allen's remarkable staying power saw off most of their hostile contemporaries, together with the Apartheid regime itself. They're now free to play Sun City as often as they like, although nobody these days lashes out the rands quite like the old crowd did. Meanwhile Mick and Tony are probably still wondering what all the fuss was about.

IRELAND! JAYSUS I LOVE YOU!

Eoghan Harris Vs. Neil Jordan 1996

For several years, Neil Jordan and Eoghan Harris had been stock-piling for a definitive crack at the Michael Collins legend. In the most literal sense, the winner would get to write history. Harris had come agonisingly close when Hollywood's Columbia Pictures gave the go-ahead to his screenplay, "Mick". Unfortunately, in 1986 the project went the way of its hero, bushwhacked in bizarre circumstances.

Columbia Pictures was owned by Coca-Cola, official supplier of sugary brown drinks to the British Army. Coca-Cola was distributed in Britain by Cadbury-Schweppes. Dominic Cadbury of Cadbury-Schweppes approached David Puttnam, the newly installed head of Columbia, and told him that the Harris film might lead to "reprisals against Coca-Cola's interests". In other words, the British army was threatening to defect to the enemy Pepsi camp. "In the end," said Puttnam, "we laughed. We didn't do the movie. No one else did the movie. It just died a death." Eoghan Harris wasn't laughing.

"Mick" went into cryogenic suspension. His day would come. Except, it never did. The revolutionary's second coming was hijacked by an imposter who looked nothing like "Mick". The plug was effectively pulled on Eoghan's moribund creation when Hollywood gave Neil Jordan the green light for "Michael Collins". Green, especially emerald green, was Eoghan's least favourite colour scheme. The slightest exposure brought him out in hot flushes. Now, he watched helplessly as his Worst Case Scenario hove into view. His beloved "Mick" supplanted by a doppleganger. A Jolly Green Giant doppleganger.

Jordan, meanwhile, clumsily surrendered an early hostage to fortune. He pledged "a very true film" which would lay bare "the untold story of Irish history". But truth is always the first casualty of Hollywood. The *Sunday Times* latched onto the "true film" oxymoron and launched a pre-emptive strike. A full nine months before the movie's release, the newspaper fired the first of many broadsides. "TINSELTOWN TAKES ON THE TROUBLES AND

TURNS A COLD BLOODED KILLER INTO A HERO, squealed the headline. The *Sunday Times* was dismayed. Collins, the paper explained, had been a "cunning... cold-blooded killer". Jordan, deplorably, was to portray him as a "courageous fighter driven by patriotic fervour". It just wasn't cricket.

By the time of the movie's Stateside release, the *Sunday Times* had worked itself into a trigger-happy delirium, comically blasting its own logic to ribbons. The paper's New York correspondent was pleased to report that "Michael Collins" had been denigrated by Time magazine as an "entertaining fantasia". Liam Neeson's protagonist, he added, was a cartoonish "bomb-throwing pin-up for terrorists". The inescapable verdict: "Michael Collins" was a mindless shoot-'em-up. Incredibly, the same writer in the same piece contended: "Another drawback for Jordan is that the film's opening clashes with the American Presidential election campaign, which means that audiences are looking for diversions from politics." Furthermore, the *Sunday Times* man detected something odd about "Michael Collins", something which persuaded him that box-office troubles loomed. The evidence: "Liam Neeson has embarked on a round of television chat show appearances in a bid to drum up business." Well, as the Yanks say, *duh*.

Elsewhere in the same organ, Eoghan Harris was opening up a second front. Jordan's movie, he carped, was "a tribal melodrama" that "fiddles the facts" and "reduces the Irish revolution to a shoot-up between cornerboys". This was not to be taken as the squelch of sour grapes. Harris explained, "To shame shoddy work is both a moral duty and a practical protection against the bomb and the bullet." One week later, in a clarification notice, Harris got in another morally dutiful dig. He wrote: "Last week I slated Declan Kiberd's invigorating book 'Inventing Ireland' and may have left readers with the impression that it was part of a tribal package which included Gerry Adams's memoir and Neil Jordan's Michael Collins movie. On reflection, I want to reprimand myself and make it clear that 'Inventing Ireland' has no sectarian agenda...".

Presumably at this point Harris hadn't seen the film, because he made no mention of the car-bomb. The car-bomb was to prove crucial to the subsequent escalation of hostilities. In the movie, four Northern Protestant policemen are blown sky high in an explosion that was beyond the technology of the day. The car-bomb incident came to light in a Daily Telegraph interview with Jordan. The director said that the scene was intended to be "funny" and "ironic". The man from the Telegraph begged to differ. He put it to Jordan that, in the context of contemporary Northern Ireland, the scene was - at very best - inappropriate and insensitive. A vexed Jordan caved in: "Maybe I shouldn't have done that, okay."

This single capitulation ceded the moral high ground to Harris. Employing his specialised knowledge of the terrain, he let fly with a sustained barrage. "Michael Collins" was "bad politics" and "a rotten movie". Jordan's artefact presented "a cheap, crude cardboard caricature of (a) complex character". Additionally, it had "no storyline" and "no woman worth a damn". Harris was furious with the Irish media for not pointing out these glaring flaws. He drafted a guide text for his journalistic colleagues: "Internationally acclaimed Irish director finds car bomb funny, then changes mind as movie crashes at box office."

It was wishful thinking. Just a few pages away from this dream scenario, the *Sunday Times* carried a report grudgingly conceding that "Michael Collins" was doing "brisk business" in the United States. By way of balance, the writer of that piece canvassed the views of the Chairman of the Disabled Police Officers Association in Northern Ireland. The RUC man hadn't seen Jordan's movie but he didn't like it. The officer added, "Maybe one day someone will make a film commemorating the lives of innocent people and maybe it will be an accurate portrayal of events." Harris, too, was gazing into a future of airborne pigs. He wrote: "Let me categorically predict that, apart from the actors and technicians, everybody who has had anything to do with making and marketing this movie will be diminished. Heads will roll at Warner Brothers."

Jordan wasn't taking this hectoring lying down. He rattled off a lengthy "comparative study" and sent it to the *Irish Times*. The subject was "Mick", described by Jordan as "a film as yet unmade, but much talked about over the past years, in particular by its screenwriter." Jordan pointed out that "Mick" was riddled with incongruities of time, place, personnel and language. He ridiculed Eoghan's efforts as base melodramatic Paddywhackery that could have sprung "from the pages of *Boy's Own*". For instance, Harris had a member of the Irish Parliamentary Party telling a crowd that the rewards of Home Rule will be whiskey and a good price for pigs. There was worse. Providing a motive for any armed individual within earshot, Collins roars into the valley of Beal na mBlath, "Ireland! Jaysus I love you!"

Justifiable homicide, m'lud.

On the "Morning Ireland" radio programme, John S. Doyle dramatised an extract from Jordan's critique. At one point in "Mick", Collins encounters a naked Lady Lavery. She greets him with a call of, "Tally Ho Mister Collins. Come and meet everybody!" *Tally Ho*, refrained John with gusto. His studio colleagues exploded with mirth and mouthfuls of Ready-Brek spluttered across the nation's breakfast tables. Harris was not amused. In fact he was livid at "the way David Hanly and Richard Crowley treated themselves to a snicker in studio." He expected no better, of course, the presenters' behaviour said "plenty about RTE's politics".

Three days after Jordan's mick-take, Harris retaliated at length. Jordan had let himself down, he wrote, by reducing "Mick" to a "sneering and self-serving synopsis". Kevin Costner himself had given "Mick" the thumbs up. In Eoghan's words: "Since Costner is careful with money, you have to ask why he paid a million dollars for my screenplay - and passed on Neil Jordan's - if there is nothing more to it than tally-ho."

Harris went on to repay Jordan's quibbles with interest. The proliferation of the "f-word" in "Michael Collins" was anachronistic. The violence was too callous. A sense of social revolution was missing. The film's failings were legion. Added together, they appeared to amount to one unforgivable fault - "Michael Collins" was not "Mick". But Jordan's film had an Achilles Heel which all could see, and Harris stomped on it with vigour.

Paragraph One: "That Neil Jordan finds it funny that...

Constance Gore Booth should shout 'tally-ho' says as much about his sense of Irish social history as the fact that he found a car-bomb scene in his film 'funny' tells us about his sense of contemporary Irish politics." Paragraph Nine: "funny", "ironic", "maybe I shouldn't have done that, okay". Paragraph Sixteen: "I am asking Neil Jordan to come clean about the car-bomb." Paragraph Eighteen: "funny", "ironic". Paragraph Twenty-two: "At the end of the day it is the car-bomb scene that sums up everything that concerns me about 'Michael Collins'."

Harris's moral victory was secure but, at the close of play, some battle weary readers - presumably including eagle-eyed officers of the Revenue Commissioners - just wanted to know about the million bucks Eoghan got from Kevin Costner. Alas, by the time Harris addressed the issue in print some weeks later, his buxom seven-digit figure had developed the anorexic pallor of a "reputed" million. Harris wrote that, after "Mick" was spiked by the soft drinks giant, "the script started again on the rounds. A series of companies went bust and Kevin Costner finally bought my screenplay out of escrow for a reputed million bucks. Warners were willing to back him on it - until 1993 they preferred it to Jordan's Evergreen - but Costner and me procrastinated because of the political situation in the North."

Yes, Eoghan, but the money?

"Alas, all of it went to American accountants."

WHEN IRISH TEETH ARE SMILING

Bernie Murphy Vs. "The Sunday Press" 1989

Life had dealt Bernie Murphy a series of hard knocks. In his mid-teens his immediate family "scattered", leaving him alone in the world. Unable to read, write or properly tell the time, his career options were limited. For years he lived hard and slept rough. Mostly, Bernie eked out a meagre living as a sandwich board man on the streets of Cork.

Bernie Murphy's fortunes took a remarkable upturn in 1985 when he was elected to Cork County Council by an emphatic popular vote. His campaign had been orchestrated and largely funded by a disillusioned former Labour Party activist, John Lennon. Murphy's successful election manifesto had included the provision of a cable car for Patrick's Hill. It would go both "up and down, as a tourist thing".

1986 was to be Bernie Murphy's *annus mirabilis*. He found his long vanished mother, he said, "because I became a councillor." A brother and sisters also materialised. His social diary bulged. Turning out for the Council in a charity football match - "Cork's Maradona" was emblazoned on his playing strip - he was sent off for abusive and ungentlemanly language. Heading for an early bath, he told his fellow players: "Ye'll be laughing on the other side of yer faces when I get elected to the Dail."

In truth, Bernie Murphy's unlikely elevation was not hailed as a joyous event by all his fellow public representatives. "The politicians were jealous," he later claimed. So it came as little surprise when Cork Corporation denied Murphy permission to attend the San Francisco Saint Patrick's Day celebrations as an official representative of the city. But there was nothing they could do to prevent him travelling in a private capacity. Bernie headed west on the trip of a lifetime.

The councillor's American odyssey wound up in the Dublin High Court in 1989. He was seeking damages arising from a *Sunday Press* account of his sojourn. The newspaper's report had been headlined "SAN FRANCISCO MAYOR ANGRY AT ALDER-MAN'S VISIT'. A number of leading lights in San Francisco's Irish community had been quoted, none of them expressing untrammelled delight at the Bernie's presence in their midst. Murphy was unhappy with the report. He claimed that it linked him with IRA fund-raising efforts. He maintained that it also suggested he'd only gone to America to get false teeth, and inferred that he'd been conferred with an honorary doctorate from a non-existent college. The newspaper denied his interpretation.

The prosecution called John Lennon as its first witness. Counsel for the *Sunday Press* noted that it is usual to call the plaintiff - in this case Murphy - as first witness. Counsel for the prosecution said he wouldn't call Bernie because he was illiterate. Justice MacKenzie said he was sure the jury would be disappointed as it would be difficult to assess the plaintiff's hurt feelings at second-hand.

Lennon said there wasn't the remotest association between Bernie Murphy and the IRA. He said that Murphy had gone to a clinic shortly before his departure for the States and had all his teeth extracted. Under cross-examination, Lennon said that in the Seventies Bernie Murphy had been irresponsible. Back then, he had no self respect and didn't care how he dressed or what he said. By the early Eighties he began to calm down and became more circumspect.

Asked about Murphy not giving evidence, Lennon said that his friend's particular vulnerability was "an inability in the instant" to articulate his thoughts. In certain circumstances Bernie became frustrated and emotional. He wouldn't be able to tell the jury what he did and where he went in San Francisco, in any chronological order. Lennon thought Bernie would contradict himself. That wasn't to say he'd tell lies, but he wasn't a competent witness.

At one point, the defence produced a photo from March '86 which featured Bernie in a nightclub. Lennon commented that it showed the alderman having a great time. This exchange drew the enigmatic remark from the judge that, "At least he has his trousers on."

Bernie and several others had travelled to San Francisco at the invitation of Warren Hinckle, an American journalist. Lennon had no idea that Hinckle had written pro-IRA articles. Bernie had told Lennon that he'd enjoyed himself in the city's Dover Club. Lennon hadn't known that the club's exterior was festooned with IRA slogans. Lennon denied that he had portrayed his friend as a simpleton. He stressed that Bernie Murphy was "ignorant but not stupid."

Taking the stand, photographer Billy MacGill refuted the suggestion that the councillor had been "shunned" as he marched past the Patrick's Day parade viewing stand. On the contrary, the court heard, "They cheered and clapped him. Mr. Murphy broke into a little dance routine and waved the American flag."

Bernie was invited to City Hall. Journalist Hinckle told him it might be timely to remind the Mayor, Diane Feinstein, that on a previous visit to Cork she'd offered to help raise a million dollars for Leeside. Bernie brought along a suitcase for his appointment to address the burghers of San Francisco, offering thanks for their hospitality. The Mayor was nowhere to be seen and the million bucks wasn't mentioned. Hinckle led the visitors to the Deputy Mayor's office. Bernie asked for the Mayor but she wasn't there. On the way out, empty handed, they met an NBC crew covering a different event. Hinckle drummed up an interview. The felicitations of the former sandwich-board man were transmitted coast-to-coast across the United States.

Photographer MacGill was asked wasn't it true "that the unfortunate Bernie Murphy was brought to San Francisco to make a fool of himself for the private purposes of Warren Hinckle?" MacGill disagreed. He'd been unaware that Hinckle had been taking regular pot-shots at the Mayor in his newspaper column. He didn't agree that Bernie had been set up with the suitcase to embarrass the Mayor.

Counsel for the *Sunday Press* read from Hinckle's ongoing reports of Bernie's visit. One headline had proclaimed, "WHEN IRISH TEETH ARE SMILING IT'S A GREAT DAY FOR A MURPHY". Hinckle had elsewhere quoted Bernie as greeting one individual with the line, "You're late, ye son of a whore!" The *San Francisco Examiner* had also reported that: "The city councilman from Cork

City, Ireland, cannot read or write and gets most of his information about America from violence-prone television shows. He expressed fears that he might be assassinated as he rode in the parade. He figured that if the crazy Americans did it to a Kennedy they might do it to a Murphy."

The article continued, "While Murphy was waiting for his bodyguard, Dr. Charlie Tobin, the West Portal dentist, came to the bar to adjust the councilman's new teeth... 'You're looking good Bernie' he said after checking Murphy's new molars in a corner of the bar where they had set up a makeshift dentist's chair made of beer cartons."

Billy MacGill disagreed that this type of publicity amounted to "an unfortunate picture". Defence counsel produced a photograph taken by MacGill featuring the alderman in a clinch with two skimpily-attired young women. The defence wondered what the people of Cork might think of Councillor Doctor Bernard Murphy appearing in that juxtaposition. "That he was having a good time," replied MacGill.

After four days in court Bernie Murphy settled his libel action against the *Sunday Press*, accepting £2,000 plus a contribution of £4,000 towards his costs. The judge deemed that Murphy and his friends had been exploited by journalist Hinckle. "They had no idea what they were in for," he concluded. Otherwise, Justice MacKenzie seemed of the opinion that the case had ended in a win-all situation. The judge felt that Councillor Murphy's election to Cork Corporation was a good thing. He must have been a breath of fresh air. The *Sunday Press* article at the centre of the case was clever, sincere and well-written. Councillor Murphy's good name had been re-established.

The wisdom of keeping Bernie Murphy off the witness stand can perhaps be gauged by some comments he made shortly after his return from San Francisco. Producing a photograph of a weightlifter named Nancy, the councillor sought the approval of one interviewer for his American sweetheart. "What about getting up that one!?" he enthused. "I didn't get any jiggy-jig," he added, putting the blame for that on Nancy's vigilant boyfriend. On another occasion he confessed his disappointment at "not scoring" on the night of his election.

Bernie had had a ball on his American odyssey. He triumphantly recalled that his fellow councillors, "thought the Yanks were making a fool of me, but they weren't. They gave me teeth. They gave me a doctorate degree." He had done his bit to maintain high standards in politics. He explained, with evident pride, "I met a lot of punk rockers in America. They wanted me to go up and stay with them, but I'd say I'd end up smoking grass and all if I did."

IT TASTED LIKE WAXY PAPER BOILED

Gerry Ryan & Co. Vs. A Cute Little Lamb 1987

"If there's any blood coming out of that lamb I'd advise you to drink it." The bloodthirsty utterance came from one Gerry Ryan, a Radio 2 nightshift deejay. Ryan's ability to spin a yarn had landed him the lead role in a real-life radio soap. He was a natural. So darn good, in fact, that pretty soon the yarn was spinning a twister-like swathe through the affairs of the nation.

It was the early summer of 1987. The producer of Radio One's flagship programme, "The Gay Byrne Show", thought it would be a neat idea to abandon a bunch of city-slickers in a remote Connemara valley with just an SAS survival manual for guidance. The nation listened in rapt attention as a sorry tale of deprivation, disappointment and disunity unravelled in daily episodes.

The sextet entered the Inagh Valley on a quest for self-realisation, big ratings and a share-out of nature's ample bounty. The SAS booklet had primed them with enticing visions. Trout from the surrounding streams and freshly snared rabbit would crackle over blazing fires. Alas, it was an infernal Artist's Impression. The rabbits were infuriatingly stand-offish. The fishing tackle snagged terminally on day one. The only things biting were dense clouds of tormenting midges. Gerry and his cousin Ciaran, a pianist, went hunting with rudimentary spears. They eventually settled for fern soup. "It tasted like waxy paper boiled," grimaced Ryan. The brackish broth was augmented with tiny minnows gulped down alive. On Monday evening Phyllis and Jean granted themselves a temporary derogation from the rules. The derring duo broke into a henhouse and poached themselves a square meal.

The six were not operating as a team. So Gerry and Ciaran were unaware that Phylis and Jean had saved some leftovers. Had they known, they might have passed up Tuesday morning's breakfast of black slugs. From now on, they all agreed, teamwork would be their watchword. In Wednesday's dispatch to Gaybo, Gerry came good with a stirring tale of common purpose. The group had fanned out through the gorse, eventually separating a lamb from its mother. Ciaran had clubbed the wee thing into oblivion with a big swinging rock in his sock. Cathleen had slit its throat with a sheath knife. Man United 1 - Untamed Wilderness 0.

Back at Montrose the phones started hopping. People were genuinely appalled by Gerry's narrative. Producer Philip Kamph assured listeners that the lamb's owner had been adequately recompensed. It was a hasty sidestep on treacherous ground. The affair went into freefall from drama to crisis. Meanwhile, the survivalists carried on regardless. They had pressing problems of their own. Eaten meat was soon forgotten and Thursday's report to Gay evoked a grim tableau of rumbling stomachs and grumbling survivalists. "The group's falling apart," muttered Gerry. The task in hand was to reach an island in Kilkieran Bay. The lure was a cache of food. Canoes were provided, but five of the six were inexperienced canoeists. Philip Kamph had supplied enough construction material to bind the flimsy vessels together into a raft. This would enable the whole group to reach the food together in relative safety.

The all-for-one raft proposal was outvoted. Phyllis and Jean felt betrayed by the others. The water was choppy. Phyllis got the jitters. Choosing hunger over drowning, she made haste back to shore. Jean was soon all at sea and the on-hand rescue service deposited her back on terra firma. The pair now faced a long walk late into the night to reach their final rendezvous. The next morning Phyllis and Jean complained bitterly to Gay Byrne about their abandonment. Their angry outburst wrapped up a week of bitchin' good radio. Nobody could foresee that the one decent meal enjoyed by the famished campers would keep repeating on them.

Disturbed by the animal's cruel fate, Dublin TD Tony Gregory tabled a Dail question to the Minister of Justice. The Minister made inquiries. He was happy to tell the House that reports of the lamb's death had been greatly exaggerated by Gerry Ryan. In fact, the ravenous hunters had met a woman named Ann Meis while traipsing across her land. Pick a lamb, she'd said, any lamb. Ann's husband shot the chosen one. She then butchered it ready for cooking. A *Sunday Tribune* photographer was in attendance the following day to authenticate the succulence of the group's triumph over nature.

The Minister's revelation caused consternation in RTE. The station issued a statement regretting the "confusion" that had arisen. RTE accepted that there were two widely divergent accounts of what had befallen the lamb, but the station was not, at present, "in a position to comment further." RTE's news department sought to nail their colleagues without fear or favour. They interviewed the executioner, Hans Werner Meis, who confirmed the Minister's version of events. The newsroom contacted three unnamed survivalists. Two denied being present when the lamb was killed. The third argued that the farmer's account was true, but that the story told on the radio wasn't untrue. "It was six of one and half-a-dozen of the other," she said.

Unlike the unfortunate lamb, the "Lambo" crisis now had a lifeforce of its own. It escalated further when a filmed attempt to corner Ryan was axed from the "Newsnight" television programme without explanation. The next day it emerged that the Director General had ordered the cutlet. RTE eventually issued a statement notable chiefly for its mastery of The Bleeding Obvious. It simply acknowledged that "misleading the public on aspects of the project is unacceptable to RTE and is regretted. Urgent action is being taken to ensure that such projects, if undertaken in the future, will be strictly controlled and accurately reported."

"Lambo" fever swept through the letters pages of the national press, providing a fleece of convenience for all comers. For some, the affair was proof positive that Tony Gregory was a malcontent, "wasting Dail time and the time of the gardai". For others it underlined the need for the Department of Health "to publicise the proven fact that meat eaters are likely to spend longer terms in hospital and to die at a younger age than their vegetarian counterparts." Meanwhile, the Kilkenny branch of the Irish Council Against Blood Sports warned the RTE Authority that the account of the killing constituted an incitement to crime.

In the heel of the one-sided hunt, the sacrificial lamb died for a greater good. Gerry Ryan's theatrical piece of bah-bah humbug was the making of him. It's said that, to this very day, the image of his late four-legged friend gambols serenely on his personal stationary.

HIS HEAD WAS ONLY INCHES ABOVE THE BENCH

The Sandman Vs. Justice John O'Connor 1978

The fate of four men hung in the balance and the judge was sound asleep. Not all the time, but far too much for the defence's liking. Justice O'Connor did his best to stay with the plot, but it was a hard slog through the dense undergrowth of tedious legal tangles, and the muggy air of a packed courtroom sapped the senses. The judge tended to flag particularly badly either side of lunchtime.

It was early 1978. Justice John O'Connor was sitting in judgement of four men charged with one of the biggest robberies in the history of the state. Nicky Kelly, Osgur Breathnach, Mick Plunkett and Brian McNally maintained their complete innocence in relation to the 1976 Sallins mail train robbery. The men insisted that they'd been mistreated in Garda custody and fitted up with off-the-peg confessions. Long prison sentences awaited the men if found guilty. There was no jury, just three judges. And one of those judges was dozing impartially through procedural quibbles and crucial evidence alike.

The defence lawyers were caught in a bind. There was no precedent for confronting a judge with his mortal foibles. Besides, barristers and judges are interfacing parts of a tight-knit druidic caste. Pointing the finger in open court would flout every unwritten rule in the etiquette book.

A solution seemed to present itself when *Hibernia* magazine published a court report mentioning the unmentionable. Buried in the middle of a drably dressed article was the sensational revelation that "Justice John O'Connor seemed to fall asleep on Wednesday last… At 2.42 pm his head was only inches above the bench… At 3.10 pm his head seems to be actually resting on the bench but two minutes later he again sits up." There was no further elaboration, no open criticism of the judge. Nobody at *Hibernia* especially wanted to be charged with contempt of court. Lawyers for the four accused hoped that the *Hibernia* report would force presiding judge McMahon to address the matter of his sleeping partner. It didn't. The disturbing allegations were blithely ignored by the judiciary and national media alike. The judge was tucked up snug in an official blanket of silence. Meanwhile, the case degenerated into low farce.

Rather than risk a direct putsch against Justice O'Connor, the defence team attempted to flush him out. Literally. They'd seek adjournments for toilet breaks, although the real aim was to rouse the judge. Other ploys included dropping and shutting heavy law books and feigning all manner of bronchial complaints. Court officials were enlisted to slam doors, bang furniture and otherwise subtract from Justice O'Connor's forty winks. Judges McMahon and Garavan sat unperturbed in the eye of this choreographed whirl.

The trial trudged slowly along, on its way to becoming the most expensive in the state's history. Judge O'Connor's ever deepening slumbers were making a daily mockery of the proceedings. The accused men finally got their way, and their barristers agreed to confront the judges. The defence lawyers privately informed the bench that if no remedial action was taken they'd be reluctantly forced to raise the matter in open court. No action was taken.

Two independent witnesses supplied the defence with sworn statements saying they'd seen Justice O'Connor sleeping. Reporters from the national newspapers declined to weigh in with collaborating evidence. One explained that he didn't want to fall out with the Gardai. The four accused were associated with the IRSP, a republican splinter group with links to the paramilitary INLA. They didn't enjoy widespread public sympathy. The scandal continued to go unreported by all the mainstream media outlets.

The trial was almost three months old when defence counsel Seamus Sorohan applied for its abandonment. He told the three judges that the application was a source of deep embarrassment to him. Justice McMahon agreed that the judges would consider their position. He did not want the defence presenting the court with evidence of Judge O'Connor's alleged siestas. That, he said, would be "unattractive".

Counsel for the prosecution objected strongly to a retrial. They pointed out that the *Hibernia* article had appeared over six weeks previously - why did Sorohan and MacEntee wait until now, the fiftieth day of the trial, to raise the supposed problem?

The three judges threw out the application. Justice McMahon stated that "the court is satisfied that no grounds exist for suggesting that justice was not seen to be done in the course of this trial." The defence next went to the High Court where they presented Justice Thomas Finlay with eight sworn affidavits detailing Justice O'Connor's derelictions of duty. The contents didn't cut much ice with Justice Finlay. He rejected the application. One reason he gave for doing so was that the three judges had expressed every confidence in themselves.

Sorohan and MacEntee's last resort was the Supreme Court. There, Chief Justice O'Higgins was sceptical. He wondered aloud whether Judge O'Connor had been asleep at all. He said that as far as he could see, the affidavits contained personal opinions that the judge seemed to be asleep. Not so, said MacEntee, the affidavits stated clearly that the judge was asleep. One of them contained the note, made near the start of the trial: "Judge O'Connor fast asleep - head on bench". After some heated exchanges, Supreme Court Judge O'Higgins and his colleagues threw out the application for a retrial. Again, one of the main reasons given was that the three original judges had ruled in favour of themselves, and it wasn't for an outside court to argue with them.

The case continued with Judge O'Connor a virtual passenger on the bench. *Hibernia* paid another visit to the court and witnessed the judge slipping forward in his seat. The *Hibernia* reporter detected a chain reaction, with District Justice Garavan appearing to nudge Judge McMahon who, in turn, "seemed to make an unsuccessful effort to rouse O'Connor".

At this point defence counsel MacEntee called for a short recess. When it ended, one of the accused, Mick Plunkett, let out a screech from the dock. The adjournment, he shouted, had been "a ruse" to enable the judge be woken up. Judge McMahon told Plunkett he had no right to speak. Plunkett repeated the accusation. He wanted it on the court record. And still the case continued.

The waking nightmare of the sleeping judge came to an abrupt end on the sixty-fifth day of the trial. Justice O'Connor did not make it to court that day. He was found dead on his bed, having finally succumbed to the weak heart which had plagued his trial performance.

For the four accused, it was all to do again.

THE COMMON MARKET APPLIED TO LIGHT MUSIC

Everyone Vs. The Eurovision Song Contest 1971

Dreary Dublin hadn't seen such fashion since Independence had brought about the passing of Castle society. The German conductor's tinted glasses drew much comment, as did the venus flytrap eyelashes of the perma-tanned lady visitors. In Stephen's Green the UK entrant set pulses racing with hot pants that could "hardly have been more than about nine inches from top to bottom". Europe's beautiful people were in town for the staging of Ireland's first ever Eurovision in April 1971. They weren't entirely impressed by what they saw. One member of the French delegation took a dim view of Dublin's restaurant culture. "Either it is very expensive," she observed, "or it is very dreadful."

When it came to organizing protests, though, the host nation dazzled its neighbours with the colour and variety of its Eurovision pageant. The tidal wave of national pride which had greeted Dana's victory a year earlier had subsided to reveal a tangle of nasty snags. If its army of critics were to be believed, the Eurovision Song Contest was at fault for all kinds of everything.

A week of rehearsals preceded Contest night, the Gaiety Theatre having been "disembowelled" to accommodate the summit meeting of song. The coming year would bring a referendum on Ireland's entry into the EEC. For those opposed to Irish membership, the Gaiety would serve as a surrogate European Parliament, ripe for the storming.

Sinn Fein's protest was strictly political. Spokesperson Mairin De Burca stated that, "We want to get across to all these countries that everybody in Ireland is not for our entry into the Common Market." Conradh Na Gaeilge attacked on the cultural front, objecting to RTE devoting scarce resources to "a pop contest". The Irish branch of the Celtic League, meanwhile, berated the organizers' failure to choose an Irish-language entry. The Gaelic League - no relation - announced a march from the GPO to RTE on the afternoon of the show to protest about the time and money being wasted on "this type of thing."

The Irish Council Against Blood Sports promised to take

"a secret course of action" if RTE went ahead with its proposed interval film glamorising a drag hunt. The station responded that the intermission sequence was "in good taste". The anti-blood sports group countered that RTE were being "irresponsible" and were showing Ireland in a barbaric light. However, when push came to shove, the Council cried off its planned disruption in the cause of "national interest and prestige".

The National Athletic & Cycling Association came out strongly against Eurovision in protest at RTE's paucity of bicycle-related output. The disgruntled cyclists didn't want to risk disrupting the actual contest, so they staged a protest bicycle race around Donnybrook the afternoon before the extravaganza. Not all the protesters would be so obliging. Newspapers warned guests, delegates and journalists to expect a thicket of pickets outside the Gaiety. One report also raised the unsettling spectre of "a militant Women's Lib wing who will chant *'Rhythm and babes means rhythm and blues'* at passers-by."

The most concerted assault on Eurovision came from within the national broadcasting service. The RTE Workers' Anti-Redundancy Committee produced sufficient cribs to stock a good-sized diocese in Christmas week. For starters, the Committee likened the song contest to "the Common Market applied to light music." This, evidently, was a bad thing.

Furthermore, they insisted, "The song contest, like the Common Market, brings redundancy. In order to take part, RTE rushed into colour expense before it was ready. They spent nearly £200,000 they had not got. On Sunday morning RTE workers will have to face a black and white world as their managers attempt to get this money back by traditional means - cut-backs, bad home programmes and redundancies."

Other gripes included a lack of consultation with staff, "the vulgarity of that musical non-event" and - in the words of the *Irish Independent* - "that the contest was creating a new kind of apartheid, the colour bar." This referred to the fact that there were only 3,000 colour televisions in Ireland. So, by broadcasting in colour, RTE had elected to pander to a tiny well-off minority. The workers' charge-sheet was made available in English, Irish, French and German.

The Eurovision circus had never seen anything like the hostility that enveloped it in Dublin. Some foreign crews completely ignored the sideshow outside the Gaiety. Others, like the Swedes, built it into their coverage as an Irish running joke. At least one unprepared foreign team tried to borrow an extra camera to capture the placard-wavers. Conveniently, RTE hadn't one to spare. The Dutch were better resourced. They filmed the chanting Women's Libbers for a special report on the plight of the Irish female. The programme was broadcast in the Netherlands as a prelude to the song contest.

Adrian Cronin, the contest's Director Of Operations, stressed the "non-political" nature of Eurovision. He sanguinely accepted that it was in the nature of "left-wing groups" to protest. "This is an age of protests," he reflected. It was also an age of bomb threats. The Monday after the Contest, the *Irish Press* carried a curious story. The paper claimed that Friday's dress rehearsal had been taped and delivered into the hands of the BBC in London. According to the report, in the event of terrorist disruption, the pre-recorded dry run would have been transmitted from London. "How the voting system would have worked out is another question" the writer concluded, somewhat undermining the story.

Nobody was particularly surprised when an anonymous phone caller threatened to kidnap the UK contestant, Clodagh Rodgers. Security was upped a notch, and attention quickly returned to what the singer of "Jack In The Box" would be wearing on the night. One female reporter carped that "the well publicised 'best legs in show business' - said to be insured for an astronomical sum - proved slightly knock-kneed when revealed in toto." Clodagh's own thoughts: "Well, they're getting a bit fat." She'd be wearing a maxi dress.

The jury were warned to pay no heed to the fat content of the contestants. The songs were to be the sole criteria for success. The hopes and expectations of Ireland were riding on Angela Farrell and the instantly forgettable "One Day Love". The whole country was rooting for a respectable mid-table finish. One columnist predicted that, in the unlikely event of an Irish win, "RTE will express immense delight while it diplomatically offers the holding of next year's contest to the runner-up."

Not that Ireland seemed to be the only country that wasn't really trying. Yugoslavia's determination not to squander its GNP was evident in a dirge that might have been lifted from a horticultural handbook: *"In some other garden you are now a rose/Your boy dreams of you/Your boy is sad."* When the votes were totted, wealthy little Monaco had taken the dubious honours with a pretty singer, Severine, a memorable tune and another outdoor existentialist dilemma. The dreamy blonde sang: *"We all have a bench, a tree or a street/Where we nursed our dreams/We all have a bench, a tree or a street/Too short a childhood."*

The other big winner of Eurovision 1971 was its hostess, Bernadette Ni Ghallchoir. Everyone agreed that the 23-year-old model, teacher and linguist from Monaghan had done the country proud. Bernadette announced that during rehearsals she'd been offered a role in an Italian gangster movie. Her big screen debut would climax with her pretty face destroyed by pretend acid. She was looking forward to it immensely.

The most conspicuous loser of Eurovision 1971 was Mrs. Mary Weston. Mrs. Weston had mounted a one-woman demonstration outside the Gaiety in support of "poor widows" scraping by on £4 a week. She was dismayed that TDs had just awarded themselves another juicy pay hike taking them up to the £50 mark. Mrs. Weston's protest came to an undignified end when she was set upon by an unidentified ruffian who made off with her placard.

Ireland had staged Eurovision without a hitch, apart from the few moments towards the start of the show when a section of the audience shushed protestors who'd infiltrated The Gaiety. The trouble subsided when it turned out that the heckles were not heckles at all. The source of the confusion was merely the peculiar babble of our continental neighbours leaking out from the commentary booths. The country exhaled audibly and basked in a mood of relieved self-congratulation. Hopefully we'd never have to go through that again.

THE CHEQUE WAS RETURNED

Michael Kelly Hits The Headlines 1995-96

What becomes of the broken hearted? In the case of Michael "Milo" Kelly, that lyrical poser had a ready answer. Milo was forced to step down from the prestigious post of Ministerial Aide because of his heart condition. Unfortunately, this unvarnished truth was temporarily scuffed during a completely unrelated hullabaloo which occurred in the vicinity.

A Fine Gael stalwart from the Kerry town of Tarbert, Milo Kelly worked as a safety official and ambulance driver until he was laid low by a heart attack. Pronounced unfit for a return to work, he was awarded a state invalidity pension. As a political activist, Kelly had close links to Fine Gael's North Kerry deputy Jimmy Deenihan. When Deenihan became Minister of State for Agriculture, he brought Kelly on board as his Personal Secretary. Kelly, who was Chairman of the Tarbert Development Association, a voluntary body, took up his new position in January 1995.

The terms of a state invalidity pension expressly forbid the recipient from working for a living. So, naturally, Milo stopped drawing the benefit. But there were complications in finalising his terms of employment with the Minister's Department. After five weeks of salary negotiations, he was asked to produce certification of his physical fitness for the new job. "This unnerved me," he admitted, "and I was fearful that I wouldn't get a contract. It was at this stage I resumed drawing the invalidity pension." But the terms of the pension were clear, Thou Shalt Not Work. "I was working," conceded Milo, "but I wasn't being paid and I hadn't a contract."

When Milo finalised his contract in May, the pension monies he'd received were refunded to the Department of Social Welfare out of his back-pay. That, it seemed, was that. But Fianna Fail wouldn't let the matter lie. Milo's pension was disinterred five months later and given a vigorous ventilation in the Dail. Minister Deenihan stood by his man, whose breach of the rules had been merely "technical". Fianna Fail's Noel Dempsey retorted that the thousands of people being prosecuted for social welfare offences would be delighted to receive letters saying they were only in technical breach of the regulations. "Talk about cosy cartels," he chided. Dempsey's colleague, Joe Walsh, noted that recipients of invalidity pensions were obliged to notify the Department of Social Welfare if they felt capable of returning to work. Failure to do so could lead to legal proceedings. The deputy wanted to know if a prosecution was pending, or would the matter be quietly dropped?

Minister Deenihan told his critics that Milo's piffling error hadn't deprived the state of "one penny". While he didn't condone what Kelly had done, he wouldn't be seeking his resignation. Milo confirmed that he wouldn't be falling on any swords. He said, "I have every intention of remaining in the job because I feel that I didn't do anything wrong."

Fourteen months later, in December 1996, Minister Deenihan released a terse statement. It said, "Mr. Kelly is no longer employed by the Department of Agriculture, Food and Forestry as my Personal Secretary. His resignation was accepted. Any questions relating to this matter should be referred directly to Mr. Kelly." When the national press came calling, Milo Kelly was in no mood for a chat. "You can talk to my solicitor," he said, "or take it off *Kerry's Eye*." He'd spoken to the local newspaper in the knowledge that it would treat him "well and fairly".

Milo's message to an intrigued public was clear and simple. He had resigned his position because of ill health. His heart was at him. The decision was completely unrelated to questions surrounding a disputed Social Welfare cheque for £1,200.

Two months earlier, in October 1996, the Tarbert Development Association - Chairman: Michael "Milo" Kelly - had applied to the Department of Social Welfare for £1,200. The money was payment to cover work carried out in the district by students. They'd been employed under the Department's Student Summer Job Scheme. The Tarbert Development Association had received approval to fill twelve positions under the scheme. In the event, only two students enrolled. They were brother and sister Michael and Leonie Kelly.

Under the Student Summer Job Scheme, voluntary groups like the Tarbert Development Association could pay students a modest £600 for two hundred hours of work during their summer holidays. The workers could be paid weekly or at the end of their contract. In October 1996, the Tarbert Development Association applied for £1,200 to pay Michael and Leonie. The Department of Social Welfare obliged with a cheque issued on November 12th. The cheque's arrival sparked disquiet within the Tarbert Development Association. Questions were asked. Had Leonie and Michael actually done the work? According to *Kerry's Eye*, "It was suggested one was in New York during the summer and the second was in Dingle on construction work."

The Association met to iron out the matter. Prompt action was urged. A second meeting was held some days later, at which it was announced that the cheque had been returned to the Department, uncashed. The Association's Public Relations Officer released a statement. He said that, "On enquiry, the Committee realised that the conditions and criteria of the scheme was not fulfilled." A Department spokesman confirmed that the cheque had been returned. According to him, the Association had explained that the claim had been submitted in error.

The cheque went back to the Department in the same December week that Milo Kelly resigned as Jimmy Deenihan's Personal Secretary. *Kerry's Eye* wondered if the two were connected? No, said Milo, "I resigned due to ill health." The journalist put it to him that Tarbert Development Association had refused to sanction the payment to two workers. Milo responded that he wasn't speaking on behalf of the Association. That body's Public Relations man would speak for it. Asked to confirm that the only students on the scheme were his own offspring, he replied: "My two children were involved in the scheme. They were not paid… My son and daughter have benefited in no way from the scheme. Money had not been paid out to my children beforehand."

It was put to Milo Kelly that Michael Jr. and Leonie hadn't actually been in Tarbert during the period of the Scheme. "My daughter was in New York," he responded, "She carried out part of the work and didn't work all the hours because she was ill.

My son did work in Dingle during the summer, but not all the summer, and he worked in the scheme, but he is also at a loss." How many hours had his children actually worked on the Scheme? "I wouldn't be in a position to tell you that," he replied, "as I didn't keep the hours." He went on to explain that the Tarbert Development Committee "felt the number of hours they carried out work didn't merit full payment, and the cheque was returned."

He outlined his understanding of how the Student Summer Job Scheme operated. "I was under the impression," he said, "and a lot of people are, that when holiday time comes, if there were any hours left, you could work those hours. My daughter was ill and we found that when she would be on holiday at Christmas time she could complete the job." In fact, Tarbert is in the wrong hemisphere to be running Summer schemes at Christmas, but the man from *Kerry's Eye* let Milo's mistake pass.

He did, however, ask if the scheme allowed for students to work any hours that suited them? "Yes," said Milo, "They didn't complete the work within the time frame, but they had every intention of working during the long break in December and January. Part of the scheme we had in mind involved indoor painting. The work in the scheme also included tidying up picnic places." In December and January? Again, the reporter let pass the flawed logic.

Instead, the *Kerry's Eye* man wondered again about the hours Milo's children had actually put in. "The only problem they had," said Milo, "was they didn't have enough time. My son was helping a local man in Dingle." But surely, said the reporter, Milo's children should have been paid for the time they did put in. Say, eighty hours? No, explained Milo: "When the local Development Association had a problem with the criteria not being filled, I was anxious the cheque go back uncashed, and that was what was done." Perhaps, pressed the reporter, the Association had got it wrong and his children were entitled to a fair day's pay for work done? "You won't get me to put words in my mouth," countered Milo. "I have told you truthfully what the story was. I'm not entitled to speak on behalf of the Association. I have been hospitalised. I have a serious coronary problem."

Which is where we came in.

THIS IS NATIONAL MOOD DAY

"In Dublin" Vs. Self Aid 1986

It was the height of the mid-Eighties Aids epidemic. First Band Aid, then Live Aid, then Sports Aid, then Hear'n'Aid (spandex and big hair against want). Self Aid was a disaster just waiting to happen. *In Dublin* magazine was having none of it.

Wise men have noted that there are generally two reasons for doing things, a very good reason and the real reason. "The concert came first," observed Eamonn McCann, "The cause was attached later." The idea of an Irish Live Aid had been floating around Montrose since Bob Geldof's global megabash the previous summer. All the vital elements were in place. In 1986 a dizzying proportion of young Irish people - "our greatest national asset" - were signed to major British record labels. The rest could make up the audience. Best of all, the rotating Live Aid stage was available.

Nobody doubted the organisers' good intentions, it was just that their plan seemed largely based on the fable of the Pied Piper. McCann spelled out the obvious - this scatty attempt to attract "pledges" of jobs and investment capital was doomed. The jobs simply weren't there, he observed, and no amount of well-meaning diminished chords from Freddie White would subvert the basic rules of capitalism. State agencies spent £450m each year trying, and failing, to create jobs. At tops, Self Aid would generate an extra £7m. It just didn't add up.

Worse, charged McCann, many of the companies involved in Self Aid were actively engaged in swelling the dole queues. RTE itself, the hub of all the hubba-bubba, was targeting 320 redundancies. The causes of unemployment needed to be clearly identified. At best Self Aid was a smokescreen, at worst an instrument for diverting blame away from the bodies responsible and onto the jobless. "Major rock stars have become as lightning conductors," he objected, "attracting the energy of the urban young and running it safely to Earth." They flattered themselves that they were part of the solution, when in fact they were part of the problem.

It was in this context that *In Dublin* editor John Waters launched a swingeing attack on bill-toppers U2. The magazine's cover headline laid out the charge: "THE GREAT SELF-AID FARCE, ROCK AGAINST THE PEOPLE". Self Aid was a nonsense, Waters argued, and U2 should have known better than to lend it credibility through their endorsement. The newspapers reported that several companies had held back job announcements in order to garner free publicity on Self Aid day. The objectors were drowned out in the carnival spirit that prevailed as May 17th. approached. Paul Cleary and his Partisans headlined an anti-Self Aid gig in Dublin's Underground venue, but they were no more than errant schoolboys larking around with pea-shooters while all eyes were on the big guns parading at the RDS and Montrose.

The big day came. A chill wind blew. The heavens opened. Ireland's massed troubadours played their hearts out, unaware that their monster meeting had caused metal muthas Dio to cancel two gigs across town, with a consequent sharp dip in employment at the SFX Centre. Those Nervous Animals chugged through "The Business Enterprise (My Friend John)". Leslie Dowdall modelled tight pants. Paul Brady played a set as dour and interminable as the nation's dole queues. Van was just Van. He growled into his microphone, "If Van Morrison was a gunslinger he'd shoot copycats." No-one doubted he meant it.

U2 too were angry. About the curse of unemployment and about *In Dublin*. Bono brandished a copy of the offending organ and the crowd booed on cue. "He appeared hurt and stung by the gratuitous and ill-founded accusations that his band were partaking in 'rock against the people'", scolded *Hot Press*, who produced the attractive Official Souvenir Programme of the event.

The grand finale was an ensemble rendition of "Make It Work", the Self Aid theme song. It was awesome, but not in a good way. Feedback squalled. The singing was wildly out of tune. The seasoned performers melted into the background while lesser luminaries Deric Herbert and Philip King vied for a dubious posterity out front. Those tuned into RTE's fourteen hours of coverage at least had the ultimate sanction of the "off" switch.

The Montrose studios resembled an open-plan hair salon, only with lots more telephones. A small but glamorous army of workers awaited the expected deluge of inspired job creation ideas and pledges. One switchboard operator confided to the *Irish Independent* that a large part of her day was spent fending off cranks, simpletons and callers with a conscription fixation. Short films highlighted worthy projects around the country. Gaybo auctioned his shoes for £300 but drew the line at kissing Mike Murphy for £50. Panel discussions on the topics of long-term unemployment, enterprise and venture capital set new records for brevity and tokenism.

The highpoint of the entire farrago was provided by a schoolboy from the Navan Road. He'd produced his own comic. Where did he get the idea, asked the reporter. "From me head," he replied. Music aside, the event reached its nadir when one "Ronald McDonald" strode purposefully into the studio and pledged 25 jobs in a fast food chain where "Staff Wanted" signs were a regular part of the furniture.

At the end of the day the Self Aid totaliser had limped up to £500,000 in cash donations, a small fraction of Ireland's contribution to Live Aid. 1,332 jobs had been registered, but this figure didn't bear close scrutiny. One hundred McDonalds jobs, 150 at Irish Life and twenty in the ESB had to be nixed because they would have existed irrespective of Self Aid. One caller from Harold's Cross phoned in with an idea for creating one hundred jobs. These were mistakenly added to the total pledged.

"The figures are not a measure of success," stated organiser Niall Mathews uncowed. U2 manager Paul McGuinness agreed. "Fuck it," he said, "If Eamonn McCann thinks he was the first one to spot that this was unscientific, he's wrong… This is National Mood Day as far as I'm concerned."

So that was that. McCann and Waters had been queering the wrong pitch. The original goalposts had long since been uprooted and moved to Clondalkin Paper Mills, where they were pulped for paper plates and party hats. Self Aid's tenth anniversary occurred in 1996. It was an ideal opportunity to reassess the event's impact, maybe visit some of the firms which owed their existence to that memorable day. Unfortunately, nobody seemed to be in the mood.

THE MURDERERS OF THE CHILDREN OF DUBLIN

Richie Ryan TD Vs. Fluoridation 1962

At the dawn of the Sixties the nation's teeth were in a shocking state of disrepair. Health Minister Sean MacEntee envisaged one sweeping fix-it measure. But MacEntee's opponents were vocal and focused. To buttress his case, the Minister needed figures to prove that a crisis existed. He ordered the Medical Research Council to assess the dental infirmities of 27,000 children in Dublin, Cork, Limerick, Waterford and the counties of Kildare and Wicklow.

The survey established that the Irish Tooth Fairy had a punishing work schedule. In Dublin and Cork the average ten-year-old had six teeth missing, decayed or filled. Worse, Irish teenagers had to negotiate their crucial snogging years with one third of their teeth blighted or absent. In October of 1962 the Minister unleashed his damning evidence in a twelve page propaganda pamphlet. The publication singled out one glistening oasis of fresh breath confidence.

The nation must look to the village of Patrickswell in Co. Limerick, said the booklet. There, "fluorine is naturally present in the public water supply. In this village the children's teeth were markedly healthier than elsewhere. It is clearly necessary to make a determined effort to curb this serious and widespread disease, one which may have far-reaching effects on general health, and which imposes an economic drain on both health services and individuals."

The Minister's pamphlet was a pre-emptive strike aimed at Dublin Corporation. The capital's local authority was about to debate the fluoridation issue at a special meeting. Legislation approving the fluoridation of water supplies had been passed in 1961 but a body calling itself the Pure Water Association had stirred up an effective poisoned-well scare. The Pure Water lobby charged that fluoridation amounted to an unwarranted "mass medication" capable of producing untold horrors. The Minister harboured genuine fears that Dublin Corporation would throw out his measure.

131

In the run-up to the vital meeting, MacEntee put the Corporation members in their place. He warned that "a partisan majority in a subordinate authority cannot be allowed to flout the law and defy the Oireachtas". He demanded that Dublin Corporation find £11,000 to fluoridate Dublin's water supply for the first year, and around £4,000 annually after that.

The Minister argued that there were only two possible alternatives to his scheme and that both were impossible. One would be to treble the number of dentists in the state to 1,800 at an annual cost of £2,000,000. Apart from the expense, it would take years to train 1,200 extra dentists. Especially with the country's 600 existing practitioners fighting tooth and drill to preserve their cosy cartel.

The other alternative to fluoridation would be to improve people's eating habits and dental hygiene. Mountainous dollops of refined sugar were a staple of the Irish diet, in tea, porridge, cakes, pies, sandwiches and anything else that would bear sweetening. Toothbrush sales were dismal. The Minister ruled out getting people to take better care of their teeth. In his view, the poor mouth was an inevitable by-product of progress. As the pamphlet explained: "The fundamental cause of bad teeth is the modern diet - and this is something that cannot be changed substantially. Ireland is no exception here: all advanced countries must pay the penalties of the modern dietry and none has found a way of changing either the diet or the habits of eating, least of all among the children."

The pamphlet rubbished allegations that fluoridated water was the Devil's own brew. Richie Ryan TD was an impassioned champion of Pure Water. The Minister's report, charged Ryan, was a last desperate effort "to push fluoridated water down the throats of an unsuspecting public". Ryan believed that imbibing fluoride was a matter for the individual conscience. He argued, "The addition of a chemical to piped water for the one and only purpose of ensuring that that chemical gets into the human body to be consumed by young, old, ill and healthy alike without regard for the specific doses suitable to each individual for the alleged purpose of reducing tooth decay in children only is indefensible."

Ryan suspected that fluoride might merely delay the onset of rotten teeth. More fiendishly still, it might actually accelerate tooth decay in adults. The Minister had his statistics, but Ryan had his convictions. He insisted, "Experience has demonstrated that… adults in a fluoridated area have many more decayed, missing or filled teeth than their counterparts in a non-fluoridated area."

The night of the vital meeting arrived. Minister MacEntee had upped the stakes by threatening to abolish Dublin Corporation if it didn't do the needful. The three-hour debate was stormy. Councillor Denis Larkin derided the Minister's booklet as "the poorest attempt at documentation that he had ever seen. He went on to say that something that was good for the teeth for a certain period might not be good later on." Councillor Ryan produced what he hoped might be a clincher, claiming "there had been increases in the incidence of mongolism in areas where fluoridation had been introduced."

A vote was called. Defiant to the last, Richie Ryan taunted his opponents on the Corporation with the cry, "Let them stand up and be counted with the murderers of the children of Dublin." This provoked howls of outrage. Councillor Ryan agreed that "for peace sake" he would withdraw the remark. Sort of. His last recorded words on the subject were sulky and cryptic: "I didn't say who the murderers were. It is the guilty consciences who are speaking."

It was to no avail. The fluoridation measure was passed by a margin of 25 votes to fifteen. Dubliners' teeth began to improve dramatically, while water-related deaths remained largely confined to drownings. Richie Ryan overcame his drink problem in so far as contamination by fluoride didn't stop him from landing the Finance brief in the mid-Seventies austerity government led by "Minister For Hardship" Liam Cosgrave. Installed as the country's chief money-man, Ryan was fond of telling the plain people of Ireland to pull on the hairshirt, take their medicine and stop moaning. He knew what was best. The electorate responded by burying the administration under the biggest landslide in the history of the state.

VAN MORRISON, I TAKE IT, ARE A BAND

Ireland Vs. Johnny Rotten 1980

Such was the vile hum of Johnny Rotten's reputation that it lingered long after he'd taken an early bath from his Sex Pistols playing days. Its pungent stench got up noses even in Ireland's loftiest ivory towers. "I am an antichrist," he'd brayed memorably on the way to selling an awful lot of t-shirts. "I am an anarchist," he'd sneered. "Don't know what I want but I know how to get it. I wanna destroy passers by." Its unlikely that many copies of that tune were worn out on the Law Library jukebox, but Official Ireland got the gist. By the time the two came face to face in October 1980, Johnny Rotten had become plain John Lydon. Just like creaky, poisonous Windscale had become squeaky clean Sellafield. In the carry-on that followed, John Lydon fell victim to Johnny Rotten's success. The immortal words of Kenneth Williams' embattled Caesar captured his predicament: "Infamy, infamy, they've all got it infamy!"

The Devil's music had been dragged through the Irish courts some months before. Abroad, The Boomtown Rats were regarded as a lightweight pop combo whose mouthy singer had blagged them onto the punk bandwagon. At home, by virtue of winning approval in Britain, they were installed as the authentic voice of young Ireland. It was only five months since the Pope had captivated the daddies and mammies with his "Yong peebol off Ireland, I luff hew" soundbite. Scruffy whinger Bob Geldof and his rat pack were clearly not the type of yong peebol the Pope was in luff with.

The Rats wanted to play an outdoor gig in Dublin's Leopardstown Racecourse. Objections were swiftly lodged. District Justice Frank Johnston nailed his faded colours to the mast. Refusing a licence, the judge said, "I have to take into account the behaviour of fans at these concerts elsewhere. They have been sent to the Isle Of Wight and other places where there is nothing to break." The judge's dire pronouncement met with dismay in BBC Television's Children's Department. They'd planned to fly a group of handicapped youngsters to the Dublin show as part of the "Jim'll Fix It" wish-fulfillment programme.

The case went to the Dublin Circuit Court. The yawning cultural chasm separating the two sides was unwittingly illustrated by Peter Sutherland, counsel for the objectors. He quizzed a witness: "Van Morrison, I take it, are a band?" The case was still undecided the day before the proposed concert, for which thousands of tickets had been sold. At this late stage the Rats' lawyers discovered that the 1890 Public Health Act didn't extend to Leopardstown, which was beyond the city limits. They didn't need a licence. They'd just wasted a needless week in court.

Word of the Rats' legal victory was conveyed to the media. The gig would go ahead as planned. The next day, with the concert only hours away, the objectors were back in court with three more hopeful show-stoppers. The judge threw out the first two applications, but he found himself inclined to agree that there might be a "stampede" if the Rats were allowed unleash their primal rhythms. The judge told the band's representatives that the concert could go ahead, but only if they raised a daunting two million pounds in insurance cover. They couldn't. The gig was off with mere hours to curtain-up. The judge expressed no fears that the last minute cancellation might spark a stampede of disenfranchised ticket-holders.

If The Boomtown Rats debacle was the phoney war, John Lydon brought the Irish judiciary eyeball to eyeball with the real thing. The former Sex Pistol arrived in Dublin in October 1980 with several members of his London-Irish family. His brother, Jimmy, had formed a band, 4" By 2". They couldn't play, they couldn't sing, they looked awful. Their prospects of going a long way seemed to reside in passing the driving test for heavy goods vehicles. Jimmy Lydon seemed determined to prove that his famous brother didn't have the family monopoly on obnoxiousness.

Jimmy had lost an eye when two black persons attacked him with a bottle. They didn't like the swastika he wore as a fashion accessory. It was put to him that the loss of an eye was a high price to pay for trying to wind people up. "Nah," he reasoned, "If you're gonna get your head kicked in to wear what you want, then you're gonna get your head kicked in, 'cos you're not gonna stop wearing it, are you?" Growing up in London, Jimmy had suffered for his Irishness. He'd been taunted and assaulted. Sadly, he reckoned, racial disharmony in London was now worse than ever. Jimmy blamed the "Greeks and Pakis and Chinks." "We're overdone with them," he griped. "There's so much immigration."

Jimmy Lydon's ramshackle band were to play Trinity College on the night of Friday, October 3rd. The former Johnny Rotten was expected to join them on stage. Around tea-time, the ex-Pistol was approached for an autograph by a fan on the street. The stranger offered to buy his hero a pint. The pair entered the Horse & Tram pub on Eden Quay. The publican, Eamonn Brady, refused to serve them. There was a skirmish. When the dust had settled, John Lydon had a court appointment pencilled in for the next morning, Saturday.

As far as the singer was concerned, it was a storm in a teacup. He went to the Trinity gig, which degenerated into an ugly brawl. Back at the hotel, John Lydon drank and talked football into the early hours with other members of the entourage. The next morning, he appeared before District Justice McCarthy. The judge fixed bail at £250 but then refused to accept that sum from the band's Irish co-ordinator, John Byrne, or from the 4" Be 2" manager, Jock McDonald. McDonald's father, a resident of the Dublin suburb of Coolock, was rushed to court to put up the money. The judge asked McDonald Senior if he knew Lydon's Dublin address. The Coolock man said he didn't. He'd only just got here. John Lydon was remanded to Mountjoy Jail. Preceeding Lydon in the dock was a man who'd been arrested at the 4" Be 2" Trinity gig the previous night. He'd smuggled a hammer into the concert and applied it with force to somebody's head. The hammer-wielding thug walked out of court on a bond of £50. As the erstwhile Johnny Rotten was led to his cell, the inmates of Mountjoy paid rousing homage by singing a Sex Pistols pastiche entitled "Anarchy In Dublin".

On Monday, John Lydon stood in front of District Justice O'hUadhaigh. Publicans Eamonn Brady and Eamonn Leddy said in evidence that the defendant and his now vanished accomplice had been ejected for spitting and hurling obscenities. Brady said that he was pulled out onto the street by his tie. He claimed that Lydon kicked him twice. Leddy, referring to the accused repeatedly as "Rotten", added that the men had called Brady "an Irish pig" and a "wanker". Lydon denied using obscene language or spitting. He said that when Brady refused him a drink he'd simply asked why, was he black or something?

"Then", Lydon continued, "when I was walking out I got smashed on the back of the head. My response to the punch was to look around and then that happened." Here, he indicated his bruised cheeks. Lydon's solicitor put it to barman Leddy that he'd "completely over-reacted", thumping Lydon in the eye after going at him "stripped for action". Leddy denied it. He did, however, agree that he had forcefully punched Lydon in an unspecified part of his anatomy "above the shoulder".

Justice O'hUadhaigh dismissed Lydon's version of events. He launched into a speech, described by London's *New Musical Express* as a "customary smug, highbrow sermon", outlining his duty to "protect the citizens of the city" from "this sort of thing". Passing sentence, the judge informed Lydon that there was "a lot of indiscriminate violence in Dublin by people with drink and without drink taken, who went around looking for trouble." He was tempted to give the defendent six months in jail. However, leniency got the better of him and he'd impose a sentence of just three. The Irish representative of Virgin Records offered to put up bail while the case went to appeal. The judge refused. He eventually relented when the Virgin man produced a letter from his bank manager vouching that he was solvent. John Lydon was on the next available flight to London.

John Lydon's brief imprisonment allowed him, in his own mind at least, to become Johnny Rotten once more. Years later, when he came to write his autobiography, his brush with the Irish law had gained more embellishments than the Book Of Kells. In his mature recollection, he'd been hauled off to a Garda station not once on the Friday of the brawl, but twice, just for good measure. His English lawyer's "upper-class, twitty voice" had antagonised the judge. At one point, a brand-new BMW had been put-up as bail. Asked for an Irish address, he'd given that of his uncle in Cork. He recalled: "They wouldn't accept that either, and went on a tirade about 'damned kulchies', which is what Dubliners call people from the country."

The warm welcome which had greeted him at Mountjoy frosted over in the chill mists of time. In Lydon's revised version of events, he was saved from a fate close to death at the hands of the prisoners only by the warders' callous decision to make an example of him. He'd been stripped naked, thrown in the exercise yard and hosed down. This convinced the other jailbirds that he must be okay. Then, as chance would have it, the prison's Saturday night movie happened to open with a performance by The Sex Pistols. At this point his fellow inmates finally recognised him. They were a tough bunch, "IRA, UDA, psychopathic murderers, the lot." Presumably the IRA and UDA men had hidden in the toilets when all paramilitary prisoners were removed from Mountjoy in the early Seventies.

The erstwhile prince of punk recalled that his cell mate was a jewel thief who'd been captured when a brick he'd thrown at a window bounced back and knocked him unconscious. Lydon's sleep was disturbed when, "In the middle of the night, two warders decided to come in and beat me with trunchons. You know the way they do: 'Your blanket isn't straight!'" The protests of the other prisoners saved him. But he felt uneasy. Neither the IRA nor the UDA knew what to make of him. "I'd lost both ways because of my Irish name and my English accent," he explained.

"I learned to be vicious pretty quick in that environment," he wrote. He'd have had to learn very quickly indeed, since he was only there for two days. No, scratch that: "I was locked up for four days - felt like four years... My father flew into Ireland from London the day I was released from prison... My father's hotel room was searched by the police for IRA weapons and fugitives."

Hmmm...

And finally to the appeal against the three-month jail sentence. Despite the actual facts of the matter, Lydon recalls returning to court the day after his release on bail. "The years were going by in front of me. Five. Ten. Fifteen. I was scared." The case before Lydon's was a "gypsy woman" charged with stealing a watch.

She got three months. The gypsy pointed out in court that she was entitled to a state-provided transistor radio for her cell. She asked the judge to double her sentence on the sound reasoning that six months behind bars must be worth a television to her. Lydon had an Irish lawyer this time. This was a shrewd move. "He said to the judge, 'Hello sir! How are you doing? I'll see you later on. We'll have a game of golf.' Those were the first words out of the guy's mouth."

Ripping yarns. Rotten memory.

NO MAN OF SPIRIT WOULD HAVE DONE OTHERWISE
The Case Of The Chattel Wife 1972

The scandal unfolded in Dublin's High Court. It heaped disrepute on the doorstep of Roches Stores, part of what we are. Yet there was something disconcertingly un-Irish about the whole affair. For one thing, native wisdom had it that you didn't wash your dirty bloomers in public. But Werner Braun was a German sophisticate with no pressing regard for the pieties of small-town Ireland.

It was June 1972. The man in the dock was Stanley Roche. The fortysomething Roches Stores director was charged with "debauching" Mrs. Heide Braun at various locations in Cork, Limerick, Dublin and Germany. Werner Braun maintained that his wife and Roche had flouted the arcane law of Criminal Conversation and that he was entitled to his pound of flesh. Roche admitted the affair with Heide Braun, but pleaded that her husband had suffered neither loss nor damage. In short, Roche argued, Braun had concocted "a false offence".

As the salacious facts of the case emerged, the newspapers were sent into a tizzy. Reporting the scandal was a dirty job but someone had to do it - as discreetly as possible. The dowdiest of headlines were employed as fig leaves to camouflage the incecent courtroom exposures - "GERMAN BORN AGENT SUES CORK DIRECTOR", "HUSBAND'S ACTION FOR DAMAGES AGAINST BUSINESSMAN".

Werner seemed to have an unanswerable case. He was an "outraged" husband whose pretty young wife had been swept off her feet by the tycoon yachtsman at the tiller of Roches Stores. The court was told that Stanley Roche had "set up in style" with Heide Braun. "He lived with her and called her Mrs. Roche and she had borne him a child." Heide had been unfaithful to Werner at intervals over their ten year marriage but he'd always found it in his heart to forgive her.

At an early stage in Werner's evidence, Justice Butler's curiosity got the better of him. The judge had noticed that the Brauns' marriage certificate said they'd married in a registry office. And yet he'd been led to believe that the couple were Catholics.

This flummoxed the judge. Werner confirmed that he and Heide were both Catholics. Justice Butler kept his thoughts to himself.

Werner smelled a faint whiff of rat after Heide began working for Roche as a decorating consultant in the summer of 1970. Roche had given Heide an Austin Mini car as a Christmas present. Later he trumped this with a sporty Triumph because the Mini, according to Werner, "would not be good enough for the places she had to go" on business. Werner often didn't know where his wife was. When asked, she'd usually fob him off with "here and there".

Werner Braun learned of his wife's affair with the Roches Stores man through an anonymous Christmas card late in 1970. The missive suggested that Werner was a "pimp". It added that Roches Stores stocked the best turkeys around. The card featured Santa Claus and another figure sitting in a car. In court, Heide said she didn't think the cartoon referred to the car Roche had given her as a Christmas present. The illustration probably represented her husband driving in Stanley Roche's Jaguar, as he was sometimes wont to do.

Tipped off by the anonymous missive, Werner confronted his wife's lover. Nonsense, retorted Roche, they were just good friends. He personally wanted to come clean with Werner, but Heide insisted otherwise, "for the children". At the start of 1971 Heide left Ireland to consider her future. Upon her return she arranged to meet her husband and children on Valentine's Day at the Imperial Hotel in Cork.

The *Irish Independent* shrank from scandalising its readers with the full sordid details of this encounter. The *Independent* reported that Werner "struck her because the meeting was held in the room she had in the hotel - the physical evidence of the intercourse she was having with Roche." That was it, clear as mud.

The *Times* flirted with titillation for the sake of clarity. It revealed that Werner "went to the hotel where his wife had a room booked. In the room he found contraceptives and a pornographic book." Heide arrived and they quarrelled. Werner explained himself in court: "I told her I would not tolerate this, that she was behaving as Stanley Roche's whore." Then he belted her one. Werner's Counsel, Mr. E. M. Wood, "said that no man of spirit would have done otherwise".

Werner's chivalric image was soon in tatters. Heide told the court that their relationship had not been an exclusive one. Mrs. Braun was asked, "How many women do you claim that your husband criminally knew?" "Approximately five", she answered. One of those women was a young Dutch national named Anne Dobbe. Ms. Dobbe told the court that on one occasion she was watching television and sipping sherry with the Brauns. When the married couple retired to bed, Ms. Dobbe took her glass and followed them. According to the *Irish Independent*, "It all developed in a way she could not remember the details of, and they all undressed and went to sleep." In fact, they didn't just sleep. Ms. Dobbe had sex with Werner. It was "enjoyable", she recalled. Heide was asked whether she'd minded her husband's flagrant indiscretion. "Not very much" she replied.

Mrs. Mareoline Tenino had been Werner's typist. Her husband was a business partner of his. She told the court how Braun had dispatched her husband on an errand one morning. Left alone with Mareoline, Werner "suddenly started feeling her clothes and asked her to go to bed with him". No way, she told him. She reported his conduct to his wife. Heide's unfazed response was that, in future, she'd make sure Mareoline wasn't left alone with Werner. Later in the court proceedings, the same clothes-feeling incident was mentioned, but with the tantalising addition that Werner had "done his performance with his trousers down". The reports didn't elaborate. The readers were left to join the dots.

Heide said she'd wanted to divorce Werner from early in the marriage. He'd beaten her. He'd cheated on her. He'd recently told her that he enjoyed having sex with other women and that "he preferred this to emotional involvement". But the presence of young children had put divorce on the back-burner. She'd also feared that her own infidelities - of which Werner was well aware - might stand between her and custody of the kids.

Heide didn't agree that she had disgraced her husband. Werner's counsel tried again, asking, "You don't think it is a disgrace that he should be known in Cork or written about as a pimp?" His disgrace was his own fault, she replied. Would she apologise for disgracing him? No, she would not.

Stanley Roche explained that Heide was originally a friend of his wife, Cary. The pair had become involved when Cary was abroad in Spain. His marriage had been a "working relationship" and had recently ended in separation. He and Heide now lived together. They had an infant child. Asked if his behaviour had made Werner Braun a pimp in the eyes of all Cork, Roche said "I don't recognise it". He was neither ashamed of himself nor sorry for his actions.

Justice Butler told the jury they must view the evidence coldly and dispassionately. It had been admitted, the judge said, that a wrong had been done to Werner Braun. His wife had been seduced and kept from him. The judge said that Braun was entitled to damages.

Criminal Conversation, Justice Butler explained, had been abolished in England in 1857 but it remained a right to be availed of under Irish law. The judge pointed out, as reported by the *Irish Independent*, that: "In this country a wife was regarded as a chattel, just as a thoroughbred mare or cow, and the jury was concerned merely with compensating Mr. Braun for the value of the loss of his wife and the damages to his feelings.

"They should not set out to punish, whatever their views were on the morals of Mr. Braun, Mrs. Braun and Mr. Roche. The court was not concerned with morals and not concerned with breaches of what was the normal moral conduct in Ireland.

"If they found on the facts that this was a marriage only in name and that before Mr. Roche came on the scene Mrs. Braun was loose and unfaithful and that Mr. Braun had been unfaithful and was guilty of the sexual perversion described of him, then the damages should be very nominal indeed. Their view should be that what Mr. Braun had lost was hardly worth losing and that his feelings were such that they could hardly have been hurt any more."

After ninety minutes of deliberation the jury assessed that Stanley Roche should be penalised to the tune of £12,000 for causing hurt and damage to Werner Braun. They'd heard that Braun was a philandering wife-beater but the judge's directions were clear, Heide was his chattel and his loss must be made good.

The award was hefty, the price of, say, sixty thousand pints of Guinness in 1972. Wives leaving husbands - even bad wives leaving bad husbands - went against the cultural grain.

The public outcry barely registered a single decibel. A few days after the verdict, the *Irish Times* carried an editorial headed "THE CHATTEL WIFE". The article meekly suggested that in the light of the Criminal Conversation conviction, "it might well be that our legislators will think the dignity of women and of marriage is impugned by its retention in the list of causes." The leader-writer could allow only one - "feeble" - justification for retaining Criminal Conversation on the statute books. He wrote, "The only possible excuse for such an action is that it might tend to lessen the chances of violence. An injured husband uses the courts instead of a club." The man from the *Times* wasn't thinking of a crowded basement disco providing criminally priced rotgut wine and a shoulder to cry on.

Labour deputies Conor Cruise O'Brien and Justin Keating took up the matter in the Dail, to no avail. They wanted to know if Justice Minister Desmond O'Malley would repeal Ireland's archaic laws which deemed women to be their husbands' property. The Minister replied that, as far as he knew, the law didn't place married women in the position of chattels. He said that, if there were any remaining areas of legislative inequality, they could only be minimal. In other words, stop fussing.

At the time of the Minister's smug reassurances, the average industrial wage for an Irish woman was half that of a man. Women were barred from apprenticeships and had restricted access to jury duty. In 1972 it was standard practice amongst banks and hire purchase firms to refuse a loan to a married woman unless her husband underwrote it, even if she was working. If a husband and wife shared a passport he could travel on it alone, but she could only do so with his permission.

It could truly be said of the Ireland of the day that a woman's place was in the wrong.

ONLY A SHOWER OF WIFE-SWOPPING SODOMITES

Youth Defence Vs. The Libbies 1992

They just couldn't let a sleeping dog lie, and in the end they got bitten. A 1986 referendum had made abortion illegal in Ireland, but Youth Defence wanted it made more illegal. Their Holy Grail was a new referendum to seal a hairline crack in the existing legislation.

Youth Defence entered the world kicking and screaming in early 1992. Ethic cleansing and no dithering was their avowed agenda. Activist Mick Haughey (Dislikes: "liberalisation", "queers", "Japs") (in 1992 anyway) found words to match the heady mood of the organisation's first months. At an early social he raised the rafters of The Piper House pub with a cry of *"Tiocfaidh ár lá!"* as his fellow Defenders basked in the warm glow of moral certitude and a few beers.

By the end of 1992 Youth Defence claimed 3,000 paid-up members, although the wrinkle-count at their rallies suggested a rampantly permissive "young at heart" admission policy. Nevertheless, the movement did exude a cocksure zeal generally associated with those who are about to inherit the Earth. The elder SPUCers, it was widely felt, were running a "soft" anti-abortion campaign. One veteran fuelled this view at a media-grooming event attended by Youth Defence delegates. "Our first mistake was trying to sound reasonable," announced SPUC's Phyllis Bowman. That wouldn't be a problem for Youth Defence.

In the war against sexually related sinfulness, aiming below-the-belt had a certain logical appeal. Fine Gael's Nuala Fennell was shaken by a vociferous late-night housecall. An unapologetic Niamh Nic Mhathuna (Ambition: "To get married and have thirteen kids") complained, "There wasn't such a big deal when the homosexuals picketed the Papal Nuncio's house, we didn't see the media then."

Pro-Choice physician, Dr. Paddy Leahy and Student Union leader Maxine Brady were singled out for slanderous tongue-lashings in a 1992 interview. Asked if she was suggesting that Brady was in the pay of abortion clinics, Nic Mhathuna replied, "She has a credit card, I don't know any other student who has one". Dr. Leahy would not be an intractable problem. "He's 75 years old and he will be dead soon," remarked Nic Mhathuna's colleague Peter Scully in the same interview.

"Your job is to hijack the media,' was Phylis Bowman's advice to the Young Turks of the Christian Right. They tried, bless 'em, but the media wouldn't play ball. Worse, there were shrill allegations that RTE had turned up the volume on Niamh in an attempt to make her "sound hysterical".

The streets of Dublin promised a fairer hearing. They'd gather of a Saturday afternoon - Niamh, Mick, Peter, Jody McDonagh (Motto: "You have to be mental to join Youth Defence") and little Bethany, the plastic foetus. Together with friends and supporters, they'd brandish harrowing photo-evidence in support of their case.

Squeamish gardai would regularly order Youth Defenders to desist from their God-anointed mission. The heckles of "pro-abortionist" passers-by were another irritant. Things came to a head in the summer of '92 when scuffles broke out on O'Connell Street during a "Pro-Life" rally. Niamh Nic Mhathuna rubbished suggestions that "minders wearing knuckle-dusters" had been cruising for a bruising. "They were our boyfriends and fathers and brothers," she explained. "We felt it would be a good idea to assist the Gardai in allowing us our democratic right to voice our opinion. God, if we only had the money to use hired muscle… It must cost a fortune."

Pardon, Niamh?

Bad choice of words. She reiterated that not a single penny raised from subscriptions "church collections, cake sales and sale-of-works" had been frittered away on heavies.

But there was more to Youth Defence than ill-tempered street politics. There was travel. One expedition to Longford yielded disappointing results. Instead of the expected strong turnout of local activists only three people turned up - half an hour late - two of them children. Upon their departure, the campaigners tried to leave some foetus pics with the proposed Chairman of their Longford affiliate. The local man reluctantly declined, explaining,

"Anywhere else but not my home town. People wouldn't accept it."

Besides the travel there was karaoke, the perfect pick-me-up after a hard day's slog on the campaign trail. Undercover reporter Michael McCaughan left his bleeding heart liberalism at the hat-check and joined the conga line. He discovered that Mick Haughey does a mean Jon Bon Jovi impression. He witnessed Niamh Nic Mhatuana's stirring rendition of "Irish Ways And Irish Laws". He joined in the chants: *"Uggy, uggy, uggy. Oi, Oi, Oi!"* and *"Mac-ma-hoo-na, hey, Mac-ma-hoo!"* (To the tune of Gary Glitter's "Rock'N'Roll Pt.2"). After the pub, it was back to a free-house. The singing continued, the highlight being Sean O'Domhnaill's rousing *"Humpty Dumpty sat on a wall… Ooh-aah, up the Ra!"*

Alas, it was all to no avail. The referendum Youth Defence so craved came in 1995 and their side finished a close second. As the awful truth dawned, the mother of Youth Defence's Niamh couldn't contain her disappointment. The scene was the RDS count centre. The poor loser was Una Bean Mhic Mathuna.

"Ye're only a shower of wife-swapping sodomites," she quipped.

"And you're only an old Bible basher," responded a young man wearing a "Yes To Divorce" badge.

"I don't give a shite about the Bible," snapped the middle-aged mother-of-nine.

"You do give a shite about the Bible," the man countered.

"Shuddup you," she explained.

"You're a lunatic," he concluded.

Nearby, Una's daughter Niamh was stoical. She'd lost. "But we really can't lose," she reflected. "Since everything we said would happen will happen now. We won't take any pleasure in that, but we did warn people."

And how.

HAPPY AS A PIG IN MUCK

Big Jack Vs. The English Language

Jack Charlton was a graduate of the Humpty Dumpty school of linguistics. "When I use a word," declared Lewis Carrol's precocious egghead, "it means just what I choose it to mean - neither more nor less." So it was with the gruff Geordie. The system Big Jack brought to Ireland dismayed the purists. Time and again he'd punt his syntax hopefully down the channels, relying on bluster and aggression to grind out a result.

The cracks in Charlton's verbal game-plan were apparent from early in his ten year reign. After defeat by Bulgaria in 1987, Jack reflected, "The game in Romania was a game we should have won. We lost it because we thought we were going to win it. But then again, I thought there was no way we were going to get a result there." Minds boggled, but a run of good results, culminating in qualification for Euro '88, gave him *carte blanche* to run roughshod over the niceties of linguistic precision. Jack rechristened several of the household names he'd inherited. Paul McGrath became "John", Dennis Irwin became "David" and Liam Brady was renamed Liam "O"'Brady. Jack wasn't one to mince words, he pulverised them.

In leading the Republic to the 1990 World Cup finals, Charlton achieved infallibility. As the Republic's footballing stock went through the roof, Big Jack became a living embodiment of Victor Hugo's dictum that everything bows to success, even grammar. A grudging admiration took root across the water, with the semantic spin-off that the team were adopted as "Jack Charlton's Republic Of Ireland" (although one ITV commentator preferred "Jack Charlton's Team Of International Misfits").

Charlton was in full swash and the English language was buckling. He contended, for example, that "If, in winning the game we only finish with a draw, that would be fine." On another occasion he confounded geographers everywhere by observing that the English people "fought two wars against the Germans. We probably got on better with the smaller nations like the Dutch, the Belgians, the Norwegians and the Swedes, some of whom are not even in Europe". Then there was the admission that, "It is true that I don't write letters to people or call them on the phone to tell them they are finished. That, for me, has an air of finality about it."

Eventually, though, Big Jack's linguistic sloppiness embroiled him in a bitter war of words with a young journalist named Paul Rowan. Rowan originally set out to write a history of the Football Association Of Ireland. In its intended form, the project might have been less than riveting. But when Rowan cadged a lift in Jack's car for a round trip from Dublin to Sligo, he got the scoop of a career.

Over the course of a five-hour exchange, Charlton ransacked the reputations of several Irish soccer heroes. Striker Frank Stapleton was "a begrudger". Jack elaborated: "Instead of Frank thanking me for stretching out his career and making something of it, he fuckin' always burns his boat." He regretted taking Stapleton to Italia '90: "I don't need Frank but I took him. Biggest fuckin' mistake I ever made. I should have sent him home in Malta 'cos he was a miserable… He didn't help for one minute, he never stopped moaning and grousing. Knowing he wasn't going to fuckin' play he could have helped and joined in with the training instead of which he carried on like a spoiled brat."

Jack revealed to Rowan the thinking behind Liam Brady's humiliating first half substitution in his testimonial game against Germany at Lansdowne Road. The Irish fans, complained Charlton, "would expect me to call him up for every international match in spite of the fact that he's not quick and not playing. So I put him on display." Brady was paraded and swiftly, some would say callously, withdrawn to drive home the point that Jack picked the team, not the fans. "The Irish don't give up their fuckin' heroes easily," he remarked, "so you've really got to show 'em." It was Brady's big day but he was surplus to requirements for the friendly. "I'm not going to give up a result against the Germans for Liam or anybody," stated the manager.

Shortly after Charlton's arrival as Irish coach his youth team auxiliary, Liam Tuohy, tendered his resignation. Some said Tuohy jumped, others maintained he was shoved by the bullish new man.

Charlton had no doubts. He told Rowan that, "Tuohy just dropped me on my head." Jack gloated, "Now, with everything I've achieved, the one thing that gives me great pleasure is that I stuffed it up his arse."

When Rowan released extracts of his book to the media in late 1994, Charlton barked indignantly that he hadn't known that his conversation was being taped. Rowan responded that Jack knew full well that he was on tape, adding that out of sixty people interviewed for his book Charlton was the only one who'd looked for a fee.

The controversy abated over the following weeks until Jack rekindled it on "The Late Late Show". On the programme, he claimed he'd been duped into believing that the bulk of the conversation was off the record. As far as he was concerned, only the first twenty minutes of dialogue was for public consumption. When he realised the truth of the matter he'd tried to confiscate the tapes.

Rowan's response was some time in coming. He searched through his recordings and released an extract taped on the home leg of the Sligo trip. This, he insisted, proved that Jack knew he was being taped at an advanced stage of their conversation. He said he took this course of action "reluctantly" having being called a "liar" and a "cheat" by Jack on the television almost a month before. Incidentally, there were now just fourteen shopping days left to Christmas.

The extract featured Rowan asking Jack about his relationship with club managers. Jack replies that they've already discussed the topic. Rowan explains, "We talked about it just on that little ride around the centre (of Sligo). But I didn't have my tape on at the time." So Jack must have known he was being taped several hours into the conversation.

The following day Jack set the record straight. "Of course I knew it was being recorded," he said, "I've never denied that." In fact, his original contention was that he didn't know he was being recorded beyond the first twenty minutes. Having now clarified his position, Jack was "no longer interested" in discussing the matter. Rowan considered Jack's final words on the subject "unbelievable and bizarre".

Things were never quite the same for Big Jack after the Rowan affair. The people's deity had been shown to have feet of clay and his players reciprocated with performances that suggested boots of lead to match. Comprehensive defeats by Austria and Portugal, and a humiliating draw against Liechtenstein - more a tax loophole than a footballing power - left Charlton gawping for excuses in the wilder outskirts of his imagination. He blamed defeat by Austria on the proposition that "there was some legs missing". A sloppy home draw against Northern Ireland brought forth the novel contention that "March is probably the one month when you cannot predict a result."

This manner of mumbo-jumbo only washed while the team were winning. The red card from his employers came just weeks short of the 10th anniversary of his appointment. By way of consolation, Jack and his missus were showered with civic honours. "I'm happy as a pig in muck" he said, accepting honorary Irish citizenship. He warmed to the farmyard theme when he was conferred with the Freedom of the City of Dublin. His memorable comment on that occasion: "I think it means I can now drive my sheep over the bridge."

WE HAVE BEEN COMMITTING NATIONAL HARI-KIRI FOR GENERATIONS

Archbishop McQuaid Vs. Yugoslavia 1955

John Charles McQuaid was rarely drunk on power, but he was seldom sober. The Archbishop's intemperance was an occupational hazard of Ecclesiastical high office, and people just accepted it. There were, however, occasions when all but the woolliest of his flock could tell that his judgement was impaired. On an October day in 1955, over twenty thousand people turned out to let Ireland's most powerful cleric know that he was over the limit.

Throughout the middle decades of the Twentieth Century, politicians of all hues poured vast volumes of temporal sway into Dublin's Catholic Archbishop. In time, McQuaid developed a tremendous tolerance for the stuff. The potentate began topping up his social quota with a secret habit. Perennial Taoiseach Eamon De Valera organised the after hours sessions. McQuaid was given a codename, "A. B.", and a free hand to run a red pen over social legislation before it reached the democratic institutions of the state. Another De Valera, Vivion, witnessed the Archbishop's vision for a better Ireland at the squinty end of its range.

Vivion De Valera was made a director of the *Irish Press* while still a student at Blackrock College, one of McQuaid's personal fiefdoms. One day, the young De Valera was summoned to the cleric's room. There, McQuaid produced a pile of cuttings which he'd snipped out of the *Irish Press*. They were mostly front page adverts for Clery's department store. The Archbishop wanted the adverts stopped. The offending items were line-drawings of women, illustrating the armour-plated underwear of the day. McQuaid gravely informed De Valera that - with the use of a magnifying glass - it was possible to make out the shape of a lady's, eh, you know, rude bits.

Between attending to the spiritual and political running of the country, Archbishop McQuaid didn't have much time for sports. And certainly not foreign games like soccer. Because of this, His Grace didn't learn about a visit by the Yugoslav national team until a few days before the scheduled Dalymount Park kick-off. It was 1955 and the Cold War was threatening to deepen into an Ice Age. The Archbishop's request that the game be abandoned wasn't the first spanner in the works, but it was by far the weightiest.

The friendly match was set for Wednesday, October 19th. With precisely one week to go, the Department Of Justice phoned the Football Association of Ireland. The FAI were informed that they'd need permission to bring the Eastern Bloc players into the country. The Association replied in astonishment that they'd never needed permission before. Visiting teams had always made their own travel arrangements. The Department wasn't interested in what happened before. The FAI would have to supply the names of the travelling party so they could be checked against a government blacklist.

More bad news was conveyed privately to the FAI. The President Of Ireland, Sean T. O'Kelly, would be absenting himself from the match. Mr. J. Wickham of the FAI met with Department of Justice officials. He pleaded that his organization hadn't exactly invited the Yugoslavs to Ireland. The Eastern Bloc team, "had expressed a desire to come, and the Association accepted." The distinction was lost on the authorities. When Saturday came, the Army Number One Band withdrew their services, this despite the fact that sheet music of the Yugoslav national anthem had been specially flown to Dublin for their convenience.

Around the time of Wickham's meeting with the Justice Department, the Archbishop's Chancellor contacted the FAI. He informed the Association's Secretary that the Archbishop "had heard with regret that the match had been arranged." The Chancellor, Father O'Regan, said it was a pity that the FAI hadn't had the courtesy to obtain the views of the Archbishop on the proposed game. It was the Archbishop's hope that, even at this late stage, the match would be abandoned. Three years earlier, in 1952, the FAI had gone cap in hand to Archbishop McQuaid seeking his go-ahead to play a Yugoslav selection. On that occasion, the Archbishop had told them he wasn't pushed either way. On further consideration, he'd suggested that the Association should consider scratching the fixture if they "could get out of it discreetly".

The Saturday before match-day, the FAI convened a meeting to discuss the escalating hostilities. Or, strictly speaking, to discuss discussing them. The Association's Vice-Chairman, Mr. L. Cleary, proposed that there should be no debate on the matter. Just get on with the game, he said. District Justice O'Riain seconded the motion. "The less discussion the better," he advised. Chairman Prole argued that, "as lovers of freedom", the FAI should open the matter for discussion. The Munster delegate, Mr. Sheridan, pointed out that most Yugoslavs were Catholics.

A vote was taken. The match would go ahead. To cancel now would ruin Ireland's good name in world football. The Leinster delegate, Brian O'Clery, wanted it on the record that if the FAI had known of any government or ecclesiastical opposition to the fixture beforehand, they would never have arranged it. He added that it would be a sorry day for Ireland when visiting players were asked their politics or religion. The only vote in favour of abandonment came from the Army delegate. The FAI decided to send the Archbishop a letter as it was agreed he was owed an explanation.

Having decided to proceed with the match, the FAI were now obliged to promise the Justice Department that they'd pay the cost of repatriating any player who overstayed his visa period in Ireland. They also had to withstand a concerted attack by the forces of Catholicism roused by the Archbishop's call to arms. The guilds of Regnum Christi said that it was a sorry day for Ireland, and so on. The Supreme Secretary of the Knights Of Columbanus complained that the FAI's decision was "regrettable". Radio Eireann's chief soccer commentator, Philip Greene, withdrew himself from the game in accordance with the Archbishop's wishes.

A body calling itself the Catholic Association for International Relations sent an open letter to the Yugoslav footballers. The missive cautioned, "You will, no doubt, be cordially greeted by the thousands of followers of the sport who gather at Dalymount Park... You will hardly guess by the demeanour of the crowd, that the great bulk of the Irish people are rather unhappy about your visit."

Another group, The League of the Kingship of Christ, issued a statement pointing out that all people are brothers in the mystical Body of Christ: "But, at the same time, we must distinguish between the state controlled Yugo-Slav soccer team, which represents a tyrannous regime of persecution, and the human persons who are members of that team." The League's point was that Ireland must be prepared to welcome, with open arms, any player who had the common decency to defect to the West. Would-be asylum-seekers must not be obstructed by "the amazing and absurd guarantee which has been forced on the Football Association of Ireland by our Department of Justice."

Radio Eireann still couldn't say whether they'd be covering the match. The station's Director, Mr. Goram, was abroad. In Rome, as it happened. By the time the Yugoslav party arrived in Dublin on the Monday night, the national broadcasting service had finally thrown in its lot with the Archbishop. The station released a curt statement: "Radio Eireann announces that it is not now broadcasting the commentary on the Association football match between Ireland and Yugo-Slavia on Wednesday, 19th instant." The visitors were met at Dublin Airport by an FAI delegation, with a cordon of uniformed and plain-clothes Gardai doing a tight man-marking job. A dismayed Yugoslav spokesman said the team had travelled to five continents and had never come across such a protest. A reporter explained that the cause of the fuss was the imprisonment of Cardinal Stepinac, an individual whose only crime was to undermine the Yugoslav state. "We completely ignore it," replied the soccer man.

Uncertainty surrounding the game mounted. There were rumours that several members of the Irish team had "cried off". Transport FC, the footballing wing of the bus and rail service, were boycotting all functions held in the Yugoslavs' honour. The non-footballing branch of the company, however, confirmed that normal services to and from Dalymount Park would be provided. The Chairman of Dundalk FC did his best to disassociate himself from any discourtesy to the Archbishop. He revealed that his club had objected to the visit as far back as the previous June. At that time, a member of the FAI council assured him that Archbishop McQuaid had been consulted and had given his blessing.

This colleague, whom he didn't name, was a liar. The Dundalk man would be boycotting the communists.

The matter reached the Waterford Board of Public Assistance in Dungarvan. There, a Mr. Curran proposed a strong protest against the FAI for inviting the Yugoslavs. According to one report: "There was a long silence following Mr. Curran's statement." This was eventually broken by a Mr. Fitzpatrick who said, "I don't feel that it is our business to do anything about that matter here today." The motion of censure against the FAI was seconded by the Mayor of Waterford.

The Yugoslav envoy in London expressed himself dismayed by the situation. Ambassador Velebit said, "It is regrettable that the Archbishop of the Catholic Church in Dublin has used the friendly meeting of the football representations of Yugoslavia and the Republic of Ireland as an occasion for a campaign of intolerance."

Meanwhile, the moral tussle had spilled onto the letters pages of the national press. One writer demanded: "Must Irish Catholics stand calmly by while the tools of Tito disport themselves and are feted in the capital of Catholic Ireland? Has the FAI forgotten the exploits of the gentle Tito, the tyrant-jailer of a prince of the Church, the leader of the mass-murderers of nearly 150,000 Catholic Croats, the kidnapper of hundreds of Greek children, and relentless persecutor of bishops, priests and laity, some of whom were petrol-soaked and set aflame with complete immunity by Tito's heroes?"

The writer continued, "The FAI will doubtless have made certain that none of the mass-murderers are amongst those with whom they propose to break bread as guests. The FAI will equally ensure that none of the kidnappers or petroleurs attempt to play with young Irishmen? No decent man would eat or play with the tools of the Balkan tyrant." In fact, the Department of Justice had already gone to considerable lengths to ensure that there was no place in the Yugoslav line-up for known mass-murderers, kidnappers and petroleurs.

There were small pockets of away support. One correspondent pointed out with evident bemusement that, less than a month previously, a team of Russian scientists were "wined and dined" by the President and Taoiseach. The writer couldn't recall a single anti-communist protest, "and certainly not from any of the people or organisations that are now kicking up a rumpus." The vital difference, of course, was the intervention of an Archbishop.

On the day before the game, the Republic's coach withdrew his services from the team. Asked why, Shelbourne man Dick Hearns replied "I would rather not say." The Yugoslavs trained on Tuesday under the watchful eye of a sizeable Garda presence. Meanwhile, the FAI were scouring Dublin for a copy of the Yugoslav national anthem to play over the Dalymount loudspeaker system. When all else failed, a group of musicians were put in a recording studio with the sheet-music sent from Yugoslavia. A special disc of the visitors' national anthem was pressed-up in time for the game.

And still the condemnations mounted. Commandant W. J. Brennan-Whitmore urged cultural purity, saying, "Since the game of soccer is an alien mode, it is part and parcel of the alien facade behind which we have been committing national hari-kiri for generations." The place of hari-kiri in Irish tradition was left unexplored by the military man. Sean Brady TD simply wanted to know, "Would it be asking too much of Dublin workers to deny themselves the pleasure of witnessing a good soccer match as an act of respect for, and sympathy with, the brave, distinguished prisoners" of Yugoslavia?

In a word, yes. In the face of the Episcopal ban, nearly 22,000 people converged on Dalymount Park to see Ireland take on the much fancied communists. The Irish players were on £30 a man, win or lose. It was speculated that the visitors would get £25 each if they won, nothing if they lost. There were other differences between the two sides. The Republic team had been pick'n'mixed by five selectors, some of whom didn't see the point of going to Ireland's away matches. The Yugoslavs favoured the new fangled Continental system of having a single manager who took a professional interest in the team.

The Yugoslavs took the field to a prolonged bout of cheering. The visitors' national anthem was accorded due respect. There was a huge roar of approval when the loudspeaker informed the crowd that, "The teams will field as announced on your programmes." The Irish trainer apart, there had been none of the feared defections. The sum total of protest consisted of a lone individual parading a Papal flag outside the ground. Just before kick-off, visiting officials politely requested that their national flag be turned the right way up as a mark of respect. The incident was as close as the Irish got to causing an upset on the day.

The cultured Yugoslavs knew too much for Ireland's hoofers. The home team stuck to their match-plan of kicking the ball hopefully in the general direction of the opponents' goal. This forced the visitors to fall back on the old tactic of pin-point passing, close control and fancy footwork. The Yugoslavs unsportingly disguised their centre-forward in a No. 8 jersey. The subterfuge bamboozled the home defence and the interloper helped himself to a hat-trick. The Yugoslavs eventually romped home 4-1 winners.

Posterity doesn't record whether Archbishop McQuaid was sick as a parrot.

EVERY NAME UNDER THE SUN

Stephen Roche Vs. Roberto Visentini 1987

The mid-Eighties were the best of times for Irish cycling. Teak-hard Sean Kelly was the undisputed world Number One, his superhuman prowess in the saddle already legend. By 1985 Stephen Roche had manoeuvred stealthily into Kelly's slipstream, actually pipping the Waterford man for third place in that year's Tour De France. Roche's 1986 season was disrupted by injury, but he did enough to show he could breathe down the necks of the world's best. As the 1987 circuit slipped into gear, Ireland's small coterie of cycling buffs had high hopes for Roche. This time the Dubliner might seal his position as the country's second top class spokesman of a generation. But Roche hadn't any appetite for seconds.

"You've got to accept that you're either going to be a super champion or a normal rider," he said, reviewing his situation at the end of 1986. "If you can't win races, you have to put yourself at the service of other riders, be a team member and help your team leader." He had a team leader, Roberto Visentini. "If you can't win races" said Roche. Big "if".

The crunch came during the fifteenth stage of the 1987 Giro Italia, cycling's most prestigious ordeal after the Tour De France. Carrera team-mates Roche and Visentini had swapped the lead for most of the previous fortnight, with Roche shading the placings. Then Roche came to grief in a Stage 10 pile-up, leaving him stiff and sore. Visentini took full advantage in the Stage 13 time trial. Back in Ireland, where cycling was strictly for kids and postmen, the newspaper headline was small but perfectly formed: "VISENTINI TROUNCES ROCHE". "My behind was killing me", moaned the Dubliner at the stage finish. He was now nearly three minutes adrift of his associate, a potential aeon in top class cycling. "I can still come back," he said, defiantly.

Few believed him. It wasn't just that Roche was several tenderised hues of black and blue. Visentini was the defending Giro champion, while the Irishman had never won a major race. In addition, Roche was shackled by protocol. As the junior partner in the Carrera team, his primary function was to protect and serve.

Besides, Visentini was the local hero. His impending victory would be good for business.

What happened next rocked the cycling world. Staking his professional future on the line, Roche stormed through Stage 15 like a man with a hornet's nest clenched between his buttocks. This was not in the team script. Visentini had drained himself recapturing the lead from Roche. He needed a rest. But now, instead of enjoying a restorative cruise from Lido Di Jesolo to Sappada, the Italian was forced into a lung-bursting pursuit of his runaway sidekick. At the end of the tough mountain stage Roche was race leader. Visentini languished in seventh place, a spent force. Oh how they booed as the Irishman accepted his victor's garland.

With one inspired piece of riding, Stephen Roche had become Italy's public enemy number one. The Italian press screamed "betrayal!" The Italian public turned out in huge numbers for Stage 16 to harass and harangue the usurper. "I was scared," he later confessed. "It was very, very frightening in the mountains. People were trying to get me. I had a police motorbike on either side on the hills, pushing people back for me to come through. Visentini was behind me and everyone was pushing him up the hills and they were spitting at me. They used to fill their cheeks with wine and rice and spit it at me as I passed."

When he reached the stage finish, Roche addressed a hostile Italian media. Visibly upset, he pleaded, "I did nothing wrong on Saturday. For two weeks now I've been racing for Roberto. I am not a calculating man. I'm a professional who does a job to the full. If it goes on like this, maybe tomorrow somebody will punch me in the eye and I'll have to go to hospital."

As luck would have it, atrocious weather and heavy security kept the vengeful locals at bay the next day. But now, ominously for Roche, the Giro course was winding into Visentini's back-yard. Quaking on the inside, he brazened it out. Visentini's challenge had exploded. The hopes of the Italian Carrera team now rested with him. He urged reason. "The team must win the Giro," he said, "There mustn't be any arguments." His estranged team-mate begged to differ.

Visentini's vendetta was now in full torrent. "He cried out to everybody that I'd gone out to ruin his Tour," said Roche. The Carrera team officials were inclined to side with their jilted Number One. Speculation was rife that Roche would be sacked at the Giro's end, leaving him without a team for the Big One, the upcoming Tour De France. The Irishman was left to stew by his employers, who compounded his isolation by slapping a media ban on him. Roche later revealed: "For ten days I had breakfast in my room, bodyguards to take me down to the start and a police escort throughout the race."

Hopelessly adrift, Visentini tumbled out of the Giro, injuring his arm in the process. As the Italian's martyrdom amplified, so did hatred of Roche. At the close of the penultimate stage, a large crowd closed in on the leader, marooning him from his police escort. At this point the story's love-interest made a most timely entrance. There, in the madding crowd, he espied Lydia, his wife. "Everyone was jumping on me and poking me and calling me every name under the sun,' Roche related. "And I turned around and I saw Lydia there and I was so delighted and so upset at the same time, because I wanted her to see me with everyone loving me, rather than seeing everyone hating me. But that saved my Tour Of Italy because I was on the verge of blowing a piston. That night we had a meal and a few words and the next morning I was unbelievable."

Stephen Roche proved himself a worthy champion of the Giro Italia by winning the final time trial in style. The imperious manner of his ultimate victory demanded respect. The *Gazetta Dello Sport* relented. "We can now call him Stefano," stated the newspaper, "The crowd has adopted him." Roberto Visentini was less forgiving. Even as Roche was accepting his garlands, the vanquished champion was wagging a bandaged finger on live TV.

Visentini very publicly dissolved his partnership with Stephen Roche that same day. His vaguely sinister final word on the matter was: "The really important thing is that where I race, he doesn't. Otherwise something really serious could happen." Carrera's millionaire boss agonised over the nasty rupture in his team. The following day he announced that Stephen Roche would be leading Carrera in the 1987 Tour De France.

The rest, of course, is hysteria.

WHO WILL MIND THEIR CHILDREN IF THEY ARE ELECTED?

The CCCP Vs. The CPP 1991

April 26th 1991, the Feast Of Our Lady Of Good Counsel, was to be a red letter day in the annals of Irish politics. The nativity of the Christian Principles Party marked a new departure back to a brighter future. Local elections were just two months away and the CPP were piously eyeing-up thirteen seats. The infant party's manifesto embraced measures to preserve the environment, the health services and Ireland's neutrality. They would staunchly foster Christian Social Teachings, "maintain the Constitution of Ireland" and oppose "Anti-Christian" legislation in any guise.

All of the CPP's candidates were first-timers, but what they lacked in electioneering nous they made up for with catchy slogans. Sean Clerkin, for instance, ran in North Dublin under a banner of JOBS FOR YOUTH - NOT CONDOMS. His personal CV outlined his commitment to women's rights, the lower paid, the Irish language and Gaelic Games. Clerkin's testament climaxed with a common touch designed to sway any Doubting Toms. "Now," it told the voters, "he is an enthusiastic supporter of Jack's Irish Soccer Team."

The CPP's campaign drew early support from the hitherto unknown figure of Gloinn Mac Tire. In a letter to party headquarters, Mac Tire rejoiced in a trinity of felicitous signs, namely the fall of Marxism, the Pope's latest social encyclical, *Centesimus Annus*, and the foundation of the Christian Principles Party. Mac Tire wrote: "*Centesimus Annus*, not condoms for children, is the true spirit of Ireland... We need not face the cross-channel tragedy of separated spouses remarrying, nor see our children pregnant before we can protect them from sex education."

Mac Tire suggested that the CPP had a leading role to play in reinventing an Ireland "of Saints and Scholars". To achieve this, he insisted, "we must all unite, although we need not, of course, become Unitarians. I would suggest the title CCCP - the Coordinating Committee for Christianity in Politics. These initials were, of course, also used by the Soviet Marxists, and their use in this new positive sense would be a rich irony for all atheists. Am I unrealistic to be so optimistic? I think not. Many would have thought Christ unrealistic though, in His own words, they would have known not what they thought."

The letter closed with an oblique reference to "some trusted cross-channel colleagues... who have a not insubstantial amount of money which could be ploughed into such a worthy venture. Neither they nor I would seek (nor, indeed, want) any personal publicity or public position - we are content that our deeds will be judged by Another. Please let us know what you think."

The Christian Principles Party were not the only ones circulated with a letter from Gloinn Mac Tire. Copies were posted to members of the Catholic Hierarchy, the Oireachtas and beyond. Bishop Jeremiah Newman of Limerick sent back his best wishes but stressed he didn't "get directly involved in politics". Nor did the Archbishop of Dublin, who suggested that Mac Tire contact the Knights Of Columbanus. The Cathaoirleach of the Seanad, Sean Doherty, responded that "what you propose is certainly an interesting idea". Doherty continued, "Naturally, I am anxious to know if you have been in contact with any other members of the Oireachtas. If so, who are they, so I could hear their views." The Vatican wrote back to say that the Holy Father had been appraised of the situation.

The tell-tale signs were there, although no-one appeared to spot them, that Gloinn Mac Tire said more than his prayers. The clues were present in the writer's deranged logic, in the CCCP acronym, in a dig at Pope Leo XIII for "supporting the British in Ireland" and in the gibberish quotation attributed to Jesus Christ. On the other hand, Gloinn Mac Tire's correspondents had no way of knowing that his moniker was a pidgin-Irish translation of "Glenn Wolfe". The name had been plucked from the "Guinness Book Of Records" where Wolfe held pride of place as the World's Most Divorced Man.

Gloinn Mac Tire was the brainchild of Dubliner Michael Nugent, and one that had clearly been touched by the hand of God. Five years earlier, in 1986, Nugent had flirted with the paparazzi when he threw his hat into the ring for the vacant position of Republic Of Ireland football supremo. The graphic designer offered to manage the team part-time on a government job creation scheme. The manager's salary saved by the FAI, he mooted, could be "ploughed into the upgrading of Dalymount Park." In the final reckoning, Jack Charlton emerged as the Association's surprise choice for the post.

If the FAI job application was a transparent caper, Nugent's invention of Gloinn Mac Tire was a prank requiring considerably more guile. He now found himself ducking and weaving in a surreal Twilight Zone where credibility and parody co-habit. With three weeks to go to the local elections, Mac Tire received a hand-written letter from the Christian Principles Party. It said, "Our printing costs to date are over £2,500. A sample leaflet for the Cabra Electoral Area candidate for the Dublin Corporation is also enclosed for your information. Our funds are now running low and any help financially from you and/or your friends would be much appreciated." Of course, Nugent's moneyed friends weren't worth the paper they were written on.

Mac Tire's response to the CPP was sent out on the newly devised headed stationary of the CCCP. The umbrella group's logo featured a shattered hammer and sickle lying at the feet of Holy Ireland, having been smote by a crucifix in a clenched fist. The letterhead echoed Sean Clerkin's election literature. "MARRIAGE, NOT SEX", it proclaimed, "JOBS, NOT CONDOMS". The officers of the CCCP were listed as "Uachtaran: G. Mac Tire. Cathaoirleach: E. O'Ceallaigh." Eoin O'Ceallaigh was the *nomme-de-plume* of one of Nugent's close associates, Arthur Mathews. Through his regular soapbox column in a Dublin magazine, the fictitious crank barked out routine denunciations of trades unions, abstract art, young people, the British, Sinead O'Connor and modern life in general.

Without actually mentioning money, the CCCP response gently ruled out any possibility of a cash contribution to the CPP's election fund. It explained: "While we hope you do well in the local elections, we must point out some areas in which we see you (no doubt unintentionally) drifting towards liberalism. Firstly, your proposal for compensation for the stay-at-home wife implies, does it not, that such a role is a chore, for which compensation is necessary, rather than a joy and the rightful role of woman. The use of the term 'stay-at-home' wife also implies that there are other wives who do not stay at home. While this is clearly the case *de facto*, it is dangerous to reinforce the concept with such careless phrases. This brings us to a more fundamentally worrying point - that several of your candidates appear to be women. Who will mind their children if they are elected?"

Mac Tire closed the subject by saying that the CCCP would encourage electoral support for the CPP's male candidates, but "cannot fully endorse your party at this point in time. We hope you understand our position on this delicate but fundamental point." He signed off with an attack on an Irish women's magazine, writing that "decent citizens should not be exposed to such organs". The suppression of women's titles, said the CCCP, would help to "revive the morally healthy climate of the 1950s."

An amended version of the same letter was sent to those members of the Catholic Hierarchy who had responded to Mac Tire's first missive. It contained a modest proposal for those bishops who'd indicated support for the CCCP but who'd said they couldn't get involved in politics. Mac Tire helpfully suggested that "a more appropriate approach would be to 'state your position' on the concept 'as is your duty' much as was done during last decade's successful referenda." The letters pages of the national press were next to yield evidence of the CCCP's divine madness. Mac Tire's gobbledygook was brazen: "From Symeon, later Peter, of Bethsaida, thrice the Master's denier yet also the rock on which his Bride was built... the Good News has not faltered in the trials of two millennia under the stewardship of near fourteen score Popes." And so on.

A body called the Community Standards Association wrote to the CCCP requesting a meeting "because of your objectives which coincide with ours, and because we belong to an umbrella organisation - COSC - which has been in existence and you appear to be duplicating it." Neither Gloinn Mac Tire nor Eoin O'Ceallaigh were made flesh, so there could be no meeting. Instead, their creators pressed ahead with their most ambitious project yet. The first issue of *Majority Ethos*, the official organ of the CCCP, was published in July 1991.

Beneath the headline "3,000 DUBLINERS VOTE FOR OUR LORD", the front page of *Majority Ethos* carried a detailed analysis of the recent local election results. The lead story welcomed the "near election" of the CPP's Sean Clerkin and Dominic Noonan as a "clear message" of warning to the mainstream parties. "Predictably," said *Majority Ethos*, "the impact of the Christian parties was even greater than expected.

"In particular Clerkin and Noonan, with their combined mandate of 2,182 votes, would have outpolled such established liberal figures as outgoing Lord Mayor Michael Donnelly (only 1,958) and Fine Gael's Jim Mitchell (a mere 1,164). In fact, even taken individually, either Clerkin or Noonan would have overwhelmed both the well known Galway Socialist and friend of Marxist Nicaragua Michael 'D' Higgins, and the English Protestant Shane Ross." *Majority Ethos* calculated that the combined votes of all the Christian party candidates in Dublin would have swamped the "meagre" total which elected socialist Jim Kemmy in Limerick. These "quirks of quotas and boundaries", claimed the mag, constituted a "clear distortion of the wishes of the electorate".

The election coverage continued inside the magazine. Gloinn Mac Tire launched an attack on the Christian Principles Party in an article purporting to call for "greater unity between the new Christian political groups". The CPP's women candidates, he argued, had cost the party crucial votes just as the CCCP had said they would. The clue for Eight Across in the *Majority Ethos* crossword was: "Amount of Workers Party members facing eternal retribution (3)." The solution: "ALL".

Copies of *Majority Ethos* were spirited onto the desks of every TD and Senator. The Dublin deputy Eric Byrne smelled a rat and, by a simple check of the electoral register, uncovered the spoof. The CCCP soon went the way of its larger namesake, but its mischievous spirit lived on. Gloinn Mac Tire was reincarnated three years later as John Mackay, "author" of "Dear John", a best-selling volume of bogus letters and genuine replies. Eoin O'Ceallaigh reverted to the name of Arthur Mathews and found acclaim as the co-creator of "Fr. Ted".

GOD SAVE IRELAND FROM INTELLECTUALS

Oliver J. Flanagan Vs. The Late 20th Century

It was a kindness that Oliver J. Flanagan expired before Irish politics was finally wrested from his kind by the spin doctors. No amount of political cosmetic surgery could have prettified his bristly red neck, nor would he have submitted to it. Oliver J. is justly remembered for the startling revelation that "There was no sex in Ireland before television". But there was more to the man than that. Much more…

The piece-de-resistance of Oliver J. Flanagan's early election strategy was a sandwich-board bearing the legend "HERE COMES OLIVER" on the front and "THERE GOES OLIVER" on the back. It was crude but effective. He was elected to the Dail by the voters of Laois/Offaly in 1943. It was his perfect year. "To be a politician is perhaps the greatest calling," he later reflected, "after the Church". He devoted his long Dail career to keeping Ireland firmly anchored in 1943. And to sorting jobs for the boys. Boasting that he'd "put hundreds into jobs", he explained, "I have always believed in working for the people and helping a friend to secure a position in life."

Oliver J. wasted no time in making a splodge on the national political canvas. One of his first actions as a TD, in 1943, was to call for stern emergency measures "directed against the Jews, who crucified Our Saviour nineteen hundred years ago and who are crucifying us every day in the week." Throwing his lot in with the Third Reich, he continued, "There is one thing that Germany did, and that was to rout the Jews out of their country. Until we rout the Jews out of this country, it does not matter what orders you make."

Ireland successfully clung to 1943 for twenty years or so. But as the Sixties progressed, the old certainties began to hurtle away at a pace that Oliver J. found disquieting. His unswerving adherence to "high standards of decency" left him increasingly isolated in a Dail swamped with Fianna Fail's mohair proto-yuppies and the pinko swots infiltrating his beloved Fine Gael. Oliver J. held no truck with excessive book learning.

In 1967, concerned to protect young minds, he laid down his objections to the new Intermediate Certificate English curriculum.

He complained to Education Minister, Donagh O'Malley, that Frank O'Connor's "Guests Of The Nation" and Sean O'Faoilain's "The Trout" contained "language which might be expected in a low-class pitch and toss school". O'Malley replied that only people of "very delicate sensibility" would find the contents objectionable. This wasn't good enough for Oliver J. who managed to have the issue listed for a late night debate slot reserved for "urgent" matters.

In the Dail chamber he quoted from "Guests Of The Nation". One line really riled him: "The capitalists pay the priests to tell us about the next world so that you won't notice what the bastards are up to in this". This, he charged, was not the proper stuff to be teaching children, many of whom were perhaps preparing for a religious vocation. He objected to the words "bleeding" and "bastards". His textual quotations brought puerile sniggers from the government benches.

This sort of language might be acceptable to Fianna Fail, he charged, but responsible parents would not stand for it. He cited other taboo expressions in the text such as "poor bugger" and "Ah, for Christ's sake". There was worse, though. O'Faoilain's "The Trout" was "most suggestive". He read aloud: *"Her pyjamas were very short so that when when she splashed water it wet her ankles. She peered into the tunnel. Something alive rustled inside there. She raced in, and up and down she raced, and flurried and cried aloud, 'Oh, gosh, I can't find it,' and then at last she did. Kneeling down in the damp she put her hand into the slimy hole. When the body lashed they were both mad with fright. But she gripped him and shoved him into the sewer and raced, with her teeth ground, out to the other end of the tunnel and down the steep paths to the river's edge."*

The Minister asked if Deputy Flanagan had read the story in its entirety. "Very suggestive," replied Oliver J., with a deft sidestep. "I did not like it," he said. The Minister continued, "Does the Deputy, if he has read the story, realise that it is in his own vivid and excitable imagination..."

"No", interrupted Flanagan, "Parents have written to me." The

Minister rejoindered, "I would also point out to the Deputy that if he had read the story he would see this young girl is going into the tunnel to catch a trout and not to catch anything else."

Minister O'Malley argued that the words singled out by the Deputy were very mild utterances. "Curiously enough," he reflected, "If preceded by the adjective 'poor' they express sympathy. In the south of Ireland if one said, 'John fell down a cliff and the poor hoor was killed…'"

Oliver J.: "If he is a poor bastard or a poor hoor he is still a bastard or a hoor."

The Minister persevered, "If Deputy Flanagan were down in the south of Ireland at a by-election, pulled up at the side of the road and was told 'John fell down a cliff and the poor hoor was killed…'"

"I would say Lord have mercy on him," insisted Flanagan. O'Malley continued, "The Deputy would say rightly, The Lord have mercy on him. He would not start slagging him for using that type of language. He would say, the poor hoor, Lord have mercy on him."

"I would not," replied Flanagan, "I would leave out 'poor hoor'. I do not care for that type of language."

The Minister closed the "urgent" late night debate with the cryptic comment: "If the mentality of Deputy Flanagan is like that of the unfortunate girl who went into the tunnel to catch a trout and not to catch anything else, may the Lord have mercy on us all."

The Seventies brought a fresh threat to the endangered world order of 1943, the fear that artificial contraception might be legalised. Condoms were more evil than bad housing, and bad housing was pretty dangerous. Oliver J. fervently held that, "Bad housing is fertile soil for communism and every other sort of -ism. Fertile soil for lawlessness, fertile soil for every kind of juvenile delinquency."

Deputy Flanagan pointed out that every vote against the condom "is a vote against filth and dirt… Coupled with the chaotic drinking we have, the singing bars, lounge bars, the side shows and all-night shows, the availability of condoms will, in my opinion, add more serious consequences to those already there. You do not quench a fire by sprinkling it with petrol."

In 1971 the *Sunday Independent* had the temerity to label Oliver J. as "the prime idiot" of Leinster House, because of his entrenched conservatism and the profound stupidity of his pronouncements. This criticism stung the Deputy into arguably his most inspired litany of sustained dog-rot. It was delivered to a Fine Gael meeting in Mountmellick.

He set out by launching an attack on the "Johnny-come-latelys" in Leinster House who wanted to legalise contraceptives. With the Jews seemingly forgotten about, he contended that artificial contraception constituted "the most serious challenge to this nation in a century". He stated, "The people who are behind the demand for a change in the law have not been elected by the mass of the people, and it is doubtful if they ever would, and the country must realise that they are new in public life and do not even know their way around Leinster House. As a matter of fact I never saw one of them (a new senator) in my life.

"The Irish people should give serious thought to what the intellectuals of our Parliament have in store for them. The demand for a change in the law in this regard is called for by professors, journalists, economists, the doctors of everything and of nothing. They regard themselves as having a monopoly of brains, ability and intelligence. They pride themselves with knowing all things for all men, but when it comes to the real essentials of life they are the most ignorant bunch you could imagine, as with all their intelligence they display great ignorance in relation to the law of God. While some of them profess to be Catholics they openly treat the teachings of Pope Paul VI with contempt, and laugh, sneer and jeer to try to belittle the advice and guidance given by the bishops of this country on a matter in which they have spoken for the good of the nation. God save Ireland from intellectuals."

Allowing himself a little pat on the back, he continued, "it is as well for the Irish people that there are in high places, a few poor ignorant men in public life, looked down on by the intellectual know-alls, but who are not afraid to stand up in defence of the law of God in a Christian country."

He denounced calls by the *Irish Times* and *Sunday Independent* "for calm discussion" on the question of contraception. There was no scope for any discussion on that issue. In Oliver J.'s version of democracy, Catholic legislators had a duty to submit to the guidance of the Catholic hierarchy. Anyone who wasn't with him was agin him. And agin God.

He asked of the *Irish Times* and *Sunday Independent*, "Do they accept the law of God? Do they accept the teachings of the Pope? Do they ignore and scoff at the advice and guidance of the bishops of Ireland, who have advised as to what is for the common good of this nation… I would like this clearly answered and none of the 'silly-billy' talk about calm discussion on a matter of so vital concern.

"Now is the time to talk, loud and clear and in strong tones, not when it's too late and the laws are passed and the permissive society have achieved the law of the jungle in preference to the law of God… No leading articles or 'prime idiot' titles will prevent me as a Catholic deputy from standing four square against all and every odds in defence of the law of God."

He wasn't finished yet. "A computer must be fed with truth and correct material in order to produce correct results, and so it is with our conscience… In Ireland today conscience can be stretched very far and is used as excuses for all things." His party colleague Garrett Fitzgerald was guilty of stretching conscience too far, he said. He noted that Deputy Fitzgerald had made a speech on the topic of contraception with "no reference to the law of God". Deputy Fitzgerald was an intellectual, the dirtiest word in Oliver J.'s vocabulary.

He blustered down the home straight. "The handful of intellectuals demanding this change can do untold damage to all future generations… I am convinced that there are outside forces at work and using these intellectuals to undermine Christianity and the law of God in Ireland."

So to the punchline. "Let us hope and trust that there are sufficient proud and ignorant people left in this country to stand up to the intellectuals who are out to destroy faith and fatherland and to replace the law of God and the law of the land with the law of the jungle. There is no such thing as a liberal Catholic... and the sooner our people realise this to be a fact, the better for success and good luck to fall upon our country."

Oliver J. Flanagan couldn't abide stretched consciences in the realm of sexual morality, but he could be surprisingly permissive in areas of direct consequence to the voters of Laois/Offaly. Farmers who were unable to get their heads around the concept of paying tax, for example, had his sympathy. He once explained that, "Tax evasion might be a sin but tax avoidance is not. And how do you know the difference? D'ya see, if you don't know the difference, how could it be a mortal sin?"

In his declining years, Oliver J. Flanagan would make regular visits to his own graveside in St. Joseph's Cemetery. "One can look around the headstones," he explained, "and think, all problems solved."

Unless God turned out to be Jewish.

THE THIRD MOST FAMOUS WOMAN IN BRITAIN

Cold Feet Trip Up Mandy Smith 1986

Mandy Smith banned by RTE. Ireland a laughing-stock, again. It was pitiably absurd and demeaning, particularly by the marginally raised expectations of the day. It was one year on from the Lesbian Nuns affair. On that momentously silly occasion, the national broadcasting service had exhibited commendable maturity in the face of histrionic opposition. If that was one step forward, this was two steps back and a cream pie in the mush.

It was late 1986. Mandy Smith was big news. The stunning sixteen-year-old had turned down the Beeb's top-rated "Wogan" show and flown instead to Dublin to make her first TV appearance. Her screen debut was to take place on "Saturday Live", hosted by businesswoman Noelle Campbell-Sharp. As it turned out, Mandy watched the show cooped-up in her Gresham suite surrounded by her flabbergasted entourage. She hadn't come to Ireland to recruit members for a gay communist whaling fleet or to simulate fellatio with a crucifix. Her party piece on the show was going to be counting to ten - *Aon, do, trí…* - like her Irish granny had taught her.

Mandy Smith's life had exploded across the front pages three months earlier with the revelation that she had been seduced by parchment-faced Bill Wyman of the Rolling Stones. At the time the furtive love affair began, she was a mature thirteen, he was a tearaway forty-seven and a grandfather to boot. Some men move their mistress into a nice apartment, Wyman installed Mandy in a swisher class of school. When the news broke, Wyman scarpered for France while Britain's Serious Crime Squad questioned Mandy and her Cabra-born mother Pat. No charges could be pressed against the wrinkly Lothario unless a complaint was filed. Three months on, none had been.

Campbell-Sharp had gone to a lot of trouble and personal expense to secure the most sought-after chat show guest in the Western Hemisphere. Mandy and a travelling party had been jetted in, limoed about and feted at the Gresham Hotel. Everything was just perfect until a phone call came from RTE saying could Mandy be in her seat by nine o'clock. But the show didn't go out until nine-thirty and it was live. The voice explained that Mandy's berth was being downgraded to a place in the studio audience.

Dubliner Maurice Boland, Smith's manager, explained down the phone just who Mandy Smith was. "She's the third most famous woman in Britain," he pointed out, pausing to let this winning hand make its due impact. Something came back from the other end. Maurice, teeth clenched: "The Queen and Princess Diana."

Boland then rang the "Saturday Live" producer, Paul Cusack. He was told he could withdraw Mandy if he didn't like the new arrangement. The producer would shortly afterwards release an official press statement saying that Mandy Smith was "not important enough" to be on the show.

Seething, indignant and bent on revenge, Boland took his troupe off to the Suesey Street niteclub on Leeson Street. They found the place strangely empty. Forewarned of Mandy's arrival, the bouncers had been overly rigorous in their application of the door policy. One person who was expressly to be allowed past the cordon was Ireland's premier Fleet Street stringer, Tom McPhail.

By Monday morning the sheer idiocy of the debacle was exposed for all to see. Campbell-Sharp was quoted as admitting that, "RTE got cold feet at the last minute. The production team had decided against her. They felt she should not give a bad example to young teenage girls. And I had to agree that by having her on the panel we would perhaps be giving her some kind 'of support." RTE's Controller of Television, Joe Mulholland, cited a "certain nervousness" about Mandy's brief history. "We did not want to go into detail," he stated, insisting, incredibly, that the late-ish night programme "is supposed to be a family show".

The "Saturday Live" Lolita-gagging botch-job petered out in an unseemly spillage of sour recriminations and disputed expense tabs, but it wasn't the last the world would hear of Mandy Smith. Within a few more years she had launched a modelling career, become a pop singer, developed anorexia, become a recluse, made-up with Bill Wyman, married Bill Wyman, divorced Bill Wyman, written a book about herself and Bill Wyman, married footballer Pat Van Den Heuwe, divorced footballer (*ad infinitum*)...

And RTE? Well, RTE gave us "The Lyrics Board".

THERE'S A BIG FELLOW CALLED SALVADOR

Fr. Michael Cleary Vs. Religious Orthodoxy

Whether his life is viewed as tragedy or travesty, religious orthodoxy was irrefutably never Fr. Michael Cleary's strongpoint. From the very beginning of his vocation he was a square peg in a round collar. Before he entered Clonliffe seminary, the "Mod Priest" in the making had instructed his Earthly father not to throw out his civvy clothes, just in case.

Young Michael felt that destiny had big things in store for him. He was going to make a difference. But how? "By a process of elimination," he later recalled, "I came to the horrifying conclusion of the priesthood. I didn't want it because it meant giving up football and girls, and I was very interested in both." He blamed the church's screening process for failing him. "I actually went in hoping I'd be found out and thrown out and I'd satisfy my conscience," he admitted, "But I wasn't found out."

Once inside, Fr. Mick gradually discovered that being a priest didn't necessarily mean having to give up football or girls. Or, for that matter, gambling or duplicity or cursing. Giving-up was not in his make-up, especially when it came to cigarettes.

In 1974 he was diagnosed with throat cancer. An operation was augmented with a course of painful radio-iodine treatment. His doctors gave him three years to live, ten if he was very lucky. He kept on smoking. Sixteen years later he marked National No Smoking Day 1990 with an unrepentantly bullish article entitled 'WHY I'M DEFINITELY NOT GIVING UP CIGARETTES THIS LENT'.

Traditional Christian teaching has it that Lent is about self-sacrifice. Fr. Michael tailored this to his own ends, preferring that: "Lenten exercises should be aimed at making us easier to live with, rather than more difficult." He backed this up with a short parable: "Some time ago I flew to Bristol. I was almost two hours on the plane and I discovered that Aer Lingus had introduced an experimental total ban on smoking on the route… Locked in a small plane up in the clouds, unable to smoke for such a period, I experienced real panic for the first time in my life. The kind hostess offered me a glass of brandy which I declined."

The offer of the brandy led the fuming cleric to deduce that: "Apparently, I could get plastered drunk and become a nuisance and a danger, or I could pop pills or shoot heroin, but I could not smoke." He further added that, "If even one seat had been reserved for smoking I might not have needed a cigarette at all." He cautioned, "We must beware of ending up like Howard Hughes - a multi-millionaire who died from malnutrition in his pollution-free, sanitised and homogenised penthouse."

Unlike his relationship with the demon weed, when it came to Catholic doctrine Father Mick could take it or leave it. He had no problem with the notion of married clergy, women priests or homosexual relationships between consenting adults. On the other hand he toed the Vatican line on contraception, claiming it rendered the sex act "as meaningless as a handshake." Father Mick was a bundle of contradictions. Or, as the blurb on the back of his housekeeper's memoir puts it, "Michael Cleary was a man of many parts."

One of his parts in particular saw a lot of action. Phylis Hamilton was unexpectedly introduced to it when she was "a confused troubled kid" of seventeen. He was twice her age and in a position of trust and responsibility. With skilful manoeuvring it became a missionary position. He told Phylis they were man and wife. It was okay to play house together, but it had to be their little secret. Fr. Mick practised what he preached about artificial contraception, and the union was blessed with two children.

Michael Cleary never contemplated quitting the priesthood for family life. He was a slave to the spotlight and his Roman collar was the crucial difference between amateur night at Butlin's Mosney and star billing at the Albert Hall. As "The Bingo Priest" he claimed the dubious distinction of introducing cinema bingo to Ireland. Having paid his dues, he gradually worked his way up the bill, becoming "The Late Late Show Priest", "The Mod Priest" and, finally, "The Singing Priest". "I was third in his list of priorities," acknowledged Phylis, "the priesthood came first, then his performing and I was last." She saw that their double life was like one of his poker games - he relished the thrill of the bluff, the risk of exposure. The high stakes amplified the buzz.

And if damnation shadowed him, salvation was always at hand. Unhinged by the throes of advanced penile dementia, he christened his member Salvador or "salvation". On one occasion he wrote to Phylis, "There's a big fellow called Salvador here and he's coming to Ireland soon. He'll stay in 'Ballyer'. I told him you would look after him well - he's looking forward to that. He's an excitable guy but I think you'll enjoy him."

Frisky Salvador contributed to a broader picture of devoted domesticity. On another occasion Michael wrote, "Believe it or not, I am washing my teeth every day for you. Sounds silly, I know, but it's like something for love. I do it for you and it's a time for thinking for you... Skippy is a bit lost, Barbie is still chasing the cars and Salvador is driving me mad since you left. He misses you terribly."

Michael Cleary played by his own rules and reached the Finish line ahead of the pursuit. He'd put one over on us. He'd made off without apology or explanation. Our loss. Phylis had once caught him in bed with another woman. He talked his way out of it. "All through his life he had a way of explaining things to make them seem normal." His explanation? It was the woman's fault.

Nothing was ever Fr. Mick's fault. His womanising, his compulsive smoking, his son's delinquency, his joining the priesthood. He swopped the orthodox clerical life of denial for a life *in* denial.

At the close of her bittersweet tome, Phylis remarks that journalist Paul Williams was "the ideal candidate to help me write a book on my life because he had almost completed another book on the criminal, the General. I was flabbergasted at the coincidence."

Amen.

Sources

THE SCREWS WERE ALL ASTOUNDED
Irish Independent, Irish Times, RTE Sound Library

THE BISHOP REQUESTS YOU DO NOT ATTEND
Irish Times, Irish Independent, Irish Press

THE MAN IN THE BOOT STOOD UP
Irish Press, Hot Press, Irish Times

A WOMAN FROM DONEGAL SAID THAT SOMEONE STITCHED HER UP
Sunday World, Irish Times, Today With Pat Kenny 28/5/97,
Joe Duffy Radio Show 31/5/97

A FAIRLY AVERAGE REPUTATION FOR RELIGIOUS TOLERANCE
Irish Times

THE PRAISE OF CERTAIN ELECTRICAL GOODS
Magill 21/3/85, Mike Murphy autobiography 1996

THEY'LL GO WILD FOR THIS IN AMERICA
Irish Independent, Irish Times

A TERRIBLE BLUNDER
Sunday Tribune, Irish Times, Irish Independent

A ROW IN THE HOUSE
In Dublin, "Into The Heart" by Niall Stokes

IT IS AN UNPLEASANT DUTY TO CRITICISE FOUL PLAY
Irish Times, Irish Independent

THE FAMILY TRIED TO STOP HIM WATCHING
Evening Press, Hibernia, Irish Times

SHRUBS WERE ALSO PULLED UP
Irish Independent, Irish Times, Hot Press

COUP D'ETAT OF THE YAHOOS
Irish Times, Irish Independent, Ulick O'Connor

I WILL HAVE YOU SHOT
Sunday Times, Star, Irish Press

THE SCHEDULE ENDED WITH 'CLOSEDOWN'
Irish Times, Hot Press

THERE ARE CERTAIN THINGS IN LIFE THAT CERTAIN OTHER
THINGS DON'T APPLY TO
In Dublin

MORAL DEPRAVITY, MY LORD
Irish Press, Hot Press, Irish Times

A FINE VINDIFICATION
Magill

PEOPLE WILL GET DRUNK
Irish Times, Irish Independent, Star

A MIDNIGHT SWOOP ON A CONGESTED AREA
Irish Independent, Evening Herald, "The Story Of Monto" by John Finnegan

THIS KIND OF NEAR THE BORDERLINE ACTIVITY WON'T DO
Irish Times, Irish Independent, "The Late Late Show - Controversy & Context" by
M. Earls from "Television & Irish Society". RTE Archive

I'M GOING TO FUCKING HAVE YOU BABY
Irish Independent, Irish Times, Hot Press, Sunday Business Post

THEY'RE A PACK OF FOREIGNERS
Irish Times, Irish Independent

ONLY MESSING
Irish Times, Irish Press, "Harried Hare Krishna" by Eoin Dillon from
In Dublin No. 318

THIS IS SPORT, NOT WAR
Irish Press, Irish Times, Irish Independent, In Dublin

ARMCHAIR LIBERALS WHO SIT AT HOME CONDEMNING APARTHEID
Evening Press, Hot Press

IRELAND! JAYSUS I LOVE YOU!
Sunday Times, Irish Times

WHEN IRISH TEETH ARE SMILING
Irish Times, Hot Press

IT TASTED LIKE WAXY PAPER BOILED
Sunday Tribune, Irish Times, Irish Independent

HIS HEAD WAS ONLY INCHES ABOVE THE BENCH
Hibernia, Irish Times, "Blind Justice" by Joyce & Murtagh

THE COMMON MARKET APPLIED TO LIGHT MUSIC
Irish Independent, Irish Times, Irish Press

THE CHEQUE WAS RETURNED
Irish Times, Kerry's Eye

THIS IS NATIONAL MOOD DAY
In Dublin, Hot Press, Irish Independent

THE MURDERERS OF THE CHILDREN OF DUBLIN
Irish Times

VAN MORRISON, I TAKE IT, ARE A BAND
Irish Independent, New Musical Express, Sounds, Hot Press, Irish Times,
"No Irish, No Blacks, No Dogs" by John Lydon

NO MAN OF SPIRIT WOULD HAVE DONE OTHERWISE
Irish Independent, Irish Times

ONLY A SHOWER OF WIFE-SWOPPING SODOMITES
In Dublin, Hot Press, Sunday Tribune

HAPPY AS A PIG IN MUCK
Irish Times, Irish Independent, In Dublin, "GUBU Files" by Damian Corless

WE HAVE BEEN COMMITTING NATIONAL HARI-KIRI FOR GENERATIONS
Irish Times, Irish Independent

EVERY NAME UNDER THE SUN
Irish Times, Hot Press

WHO WILL MIND THEIR CHILDREN IF THEY ARE ELECTED?
Majority Ethos, Michael Nugent

GOD SAVE IRELAND FROM INTELLECTUALS
Irish Times, Irish Independent

THE THIRD MOST FAMOUS WOMAN IN BRITAIN
Irish Times, Irish Independent, "Making Plans For Mandy" by Sam Smyth
from In Dublin No. 268, interview with author

THERE'S A BIG FELLOW CALLED SALVADOR
Evening Press, Hot Press, Star, "Secret Love" by Phyllis Hamilton